Sharing Your

FAITH

with

MUSLIMS

WADE AKINS

✝HANNIBAL BOOKS
www.hannibalbooks.com

Printed in the United States of America
by Lightning Source Inc.
Cover design by Dennis Davidson

Unless otherwise indicated
all Scriptures taken from the Holy Bible,
New International Version, copyright 1973, 1978, 1984
by International Bible Society.
Scriptures in The Good News of Jesus studies in the Appendix
are taken from the Holy Bible, New King James Version,
copyright 1979 and 1980 by Thomas Nelson Publishers.
Library of Congress Control Number: 2010942759
ISBN 978-1-934749-97-5

Hannibal Books
PO Box 461592
Garland, TX 75046
1-800-747-0738
hannibalbooks@earthlink.net
www.hannibalbooks.com

Dedication

This book is dedicated to my wonderful wife, Barbara. We are married both in marriage and ministry. She and I have traveled the world together as we have trained leaders in evangelism and discipleship. Barbara spent many hours working to help me with this book.

God has used her to share the Good News of Jesus to Muslims. She has done this through personal Bible studies as well as by conducting special evangelism training conferences in Muslim nations. She is a faithful partner and loves Christ with all of her heart, mind, and soul. I am privileged and honored to have her as my incredible wife. She is what I call "God's Gift of Grace".

Acknowledgements

I would like to thank four special people.

First is my daughter, Christy A. Brawner, who worked diligently as she assisted in editing this book. She teaches English in Memphis, TN, and serves Christ in her local church. She is a dedicated wife and mother and loves the Lord with all of her heart, mind, and soul. Without her assistance this book would not have been ready to go to the publisher.

Secondly, I would like to acknowledge Dr. Stan May, professor of missions at Mid-America Baptist Theological Seminary in Memphis, TN. Dr. May is the one who invited me to teach Islam and Evangelizing Muslims at the seminary. God used him to help me become more aware and involved in Islamic evangelism. I am deeply grateful to Dr. May for allowing God to use him to set me on this path.

Thirdly, I would like to thank my publishers, Louis and Kay Moore of Hannibal Books. They have been so helpful to me in my writing ministry. God is using them to publish great Christian books. I want to thank them for giving me the opportunity to work and minister with them. They are gracious and loving servants of the Lord.

Contents

Foreword

Three years ago, as I searched through a missions blog, this statement caught my eye: "Wade Akins is a master church-planter. To whatever he has to say, I typically try to listen." This post by a missionary in Central America caught my attention. In these two ways I reflected on this statement: First, *how did this missionary know Wade Akins since Dr. Akins hasn't worked extensively in the area of Central America?* Second, *is this bold description, "master church-planter", true?*

On reflection I can assure you that this young missionary's statement is entirely correct. Among church planters/missionaries from multiple denominations Dr. Wade Akins has become known as one who walks what he talks. Because they have decades of experience in those areas, he and his wife, Barbara, have been able to train missionaries and laypeople in the art of evangelism and church-planting. In the world of missions Wade and Barbara Akins are two people who merit one's time.

After a remarkably successful ministry in South America in which literally hundreds of documented churches were started, Dr. Akins began to train churches on every continent around the world. However, a focus of much of his time became the Muslim world. Through interviews with soul-winning Muslims Dr. Akins began to examine how to win other Muslims to Christ.

On top of these interviews, for years you could not find Dr. Akins without some book about Islam being in his hand. During this time of study and preparation, Dr. Akins and Barbara continued to train churches in predominantly Roman Catholic, atheist, Hindu, Buddhist, and Muslim countries. They always were on a plane to somewhere to teach for the Lord. In this time period the number of documented churches from their ministry grew to more than 10,000.

Now, after years of research and personal experience, Dr. Akins has given us this book, *Sharing Your Faith with Muslims*. In a literary world in which most books on world religions deal with biographies, timelines, and general theories, Dr. Akins has given us a PRACTICAL handbook with specific tips on how one actually can lead a Muslim to Christ. The whole thrust of the book is to take people from the theoretical to the practical so they can be confident in sharing their faith with others.

My hope and prayer is that you can take these practical ideas in evangelizing Muslims and apply them to your daily life. Dr. Akins has given us some means by which we can show Christ to the 1.3 billion Muslims who so desperately need to know that God loves them and that they are vitally important to Him.

In Christ,

Dr. Jeff Brawner
Assistant Professor of Theological Studies, Church History and Missions
Mid-America Baptist Theological Seminary, Memphis, TN

Introduction

The Challenge

Reaching Muslims for Christ is a great challenge. This book is for those who have a desire to reach their world for Christ but have no idea how to go about sharing their faith with Muslims. To be an effective witness to those reared in Islam, one needs to understand these six things:

• The founder of Islam
• The holy book of the Muslim religion—the Koran
• The basic doctrinal beliefs of Islam
• The cultural and social issues of the religion
• The basic barriers or stumbling blocks Muslims have toward the gospel
• Practical evangelism strategies that will introduce Christ to people of that religion

This book does not deal with "theory", but it is a "practical" book that will share the "how to's" about effective ways to evangelize Muslims. When readers finish this book, they will know how to approach and share Christ with their Muslim friends.

This book could have been a thousand pages in length about Islam and evangelism, but it was written for the pastor and layperson who do not have the time to spend the hundreds or even thousands of hours needed to understand everything about Islam but who still want to be an effective witness for Christ.

In my opinion one does not necessarily have to understand everything about Islam to be an effective witness. However, one must understand some basics. In a very practical way this book will cover these basics, so the reader will be well-equipped to share his or her faith with Muslims.

Evangelizing Muslims is a challenge, because if Muslims convert to Christ, they are considered "apostates" and can suffer very severe penalties that result in being ostracized from their families, communities, societies, or even can result in death.

Because of two different reasons most of us do not involve ourselves in evangelizing Muslims.

• First, we are afraid. Fear is a dominating cause that Satan can use to prevent us from sharing our faith with anyone but especially Muslims.
• Secondly, we are uninformed. We do not know anything or very much about Islam and how to relate to Muslims. I hope God will use this book to eliminate both of these factors from your life and that God will use you to share Christ with Muslims.

From my own experiences I have grown to realize that talking to Muslims about Christ is very easy. Most Muslims are very open and willing to talk about their religion. They are not ashamed. They are not shy about talking about Allah, their god. They are not bashful in trying to convert you. They are bold in their witness.

Thus, how do you approach the Muslim? How do you share your faith with a Muslim so he or she can understand the gospel? That is what this book will teach you.

PART I
THE BASICS

Chapter 1

The Founder, Muhammad

The founder of Islam was a man named Muhammad. He was born about 570 years after the birth of Christ. He was born in the city of Mecca in what now is Saudi Arabia.

What was Arabia like before Muhammad? Jews, Christians, and pagans lived in Arabia. Mecca had a local shrine called the *Kaaba*, which housed numerous pagan idols.

His Birth and Early Life in Mecca

According to tradition Muhammad was born April 20, 570 A.D. (or April 26, according to the Shiites) as Muhammad Ibn Abdullah (the son of Abdullah Muddalib). He was of the Quraysh tribe. His mother's name was Amina.[i]

His father died before his birth. His mother, Amina, died when Muhammad was 6. He was reared by his uncle, Abu Talib.

Wives

His uncle recommended for him to work for a wealthy widow named Khadija. She was 15-years older than he and hired him as a traveling salesperson to go to Syria and trade her goods. Khadija was so impressed with the fact that in his job Muhammad had doubled her wealth, she proposed marriage to him.ii

When he was 25, he married Khadija, who was 40. They had two sons, who both died in infancy, and four daughters. He worked as a supervisor of her trade with Syria. This marriage raised his social status among the wealthy elite of Mecca.iii

When Muhammad was 50, Khadija died. For 25 years he had known only one woman, who was his greatest supporter. After her death, however, he would marry other women so that ultimately he had at least 13 wives, one of whom was only 6-years old. The name of this youngest wife was Aisha; this marriage was consummated when she was 9 years of age. Muslim men are allowed up to four wives, but Muhammad said Allah made a special exception for him. Throughout his lifetime Muhammad got numerous special exceptions from the rules and laws he set up for all other Muslims.

His First Revelation

Because of their wealth he was allowed more time to visit a popular cave at Mt. Hira, which was three miles from Mecca. He would spend one month per year there. At the cave he would wrap himself up in a garment and keep vigils at night. He would repeat the name of Allah.iv

In 610, at age 40, while he was at the cave on Mt. Hira, Muhammad received his first revelation during the month of Ramadan. He claimed the revelation was from the angel Gabriel, who spoke to him in Arabic.

Muhammad believed that Gabriel was to be the medium of communication between himself and Allah. These revelations later would become the Muslims' sacred scriptures, the Koran.

One night during the month of Ramadan he was in prayer when he had a vision. He claimed that Gabriel spoke the word *Iqra*, which means "read" or "proclaim" or "recite". Muhammad responded that he could not read. Nevertheless, he recited the words of the angel. This famous revelation is recorded in Koran 96:1-5.v

This began a series of revelations that would continue off and on for the next 22 years until his death in 632 A.D. He claimed to have received 113 more of these revelations. His followers committed them to memory and wrote them on whatever was available. After his death these revelations were collected into what now is the Koran.

His Doubts

According to Aisha, later his favorite wife, Muhammad expressed great distress to Khadija because he doubted the source of these revelations.[vi] He repeated to her his initial fears, "Woe is me poet or possessed".[vii] By *poet* he meant one who received ecstatic, and possibly demonic, visions.[viii]

Muhammad was so overcome both by fear and despair, he contemplated suicide. Khadija had a cousin named Waraqa who was a Christian priest. When Khadija told Waraqa what Muhammad had experienced in the cave of Hira, he confirmed to her that Muhammad truly was a prophet and that he was not possessed by demons.[ix]

Without the care of Khadija and the aid of Waraqa, the world never would have known of Muhammad or Islam.[x]

After Waraqa died, Muhammad was so sad that he went to the tops of mountains with the intent to throw himself down. Gabriel appeared before him and said, "O Muhammad! You are indeed Allah's Messenger in truth." His heart would become quiet; he would calm down and return home.[xi]

At one point Muhammad said that Gabriel brought him *Sura* 93:1-3. After this, the revelations occurred frequently; Muhammad no longer doubted the source of his revelations.

Dr. Emir Caner finds Muhammad's doubts to be very troubling. He points out the fact that for a major prophet to doubt the source of his prophetic revelation is troubling.[xii]

His Preaching in Mecca

Muhammad began preaching in Mecca. His message was calling the people to worship the one true God, Allah. He called them to forsake their idols and to acknowledge him as a prophet.

He became a "warner". In the beginning his preaching was simple. He preached *monotheism* (only one God exists). Because of the peoples' rejection of his message he threatened the pagan Meccans with annihilation (*Sura* 21:11-15). (Observe: Chapters in the Koran are called *Suras*; throughout this book we will use this term.)

His detractors asked him why he did not perform miracles. He told them that his miracle was the Koran.

His Persecution in Mecca

In the 10th year of his mission, his wife, Khadija, died. She was 65-years old; at the time he was 50. Just a few weeks later his uncle, Abu Talib, also passed away. These were his two key supporters.

Verbal persecution began. People accused him of being a liar, lunatic, and demon-possessed. His principal persecutor was his uncle, Abu Lahab. When Abu rejected his message, Muhammad used violent language to curse him and his wife. In *Sura* 111:1-5 he referred to his uncle as the "Father of the Flame". The uncle and his wife were condemned to hell fire.

His Flight—The Hijra—
On July 16, 622, Muhammad Flees Mecca to Medina

This is the most famous date in Islam—the year of the Flight to Medina, 270 miles north. It is the beginning of the Islamic calendar, 1. AH.

This new sect infuriated the leaders of Mecca. To end the new faith they planned to assassinate Muhammad. Muhammad and Abu Bakr, one of Muhammad's first converts, along with the remaining Muslims escaped from Mecca. Along the way they hid in caves until they arrived in Medina.[xiii]

At age 53 on September 24, 622, he arrived safely in Medina. He was well-received in the area, which also had a strong tradition of Jewish monotheism.

Medina was different from Mecca. More people, including numerous Jews who lived there, believed in just one God.[xiv]

However, three Jewish tribes caused him trouble. Thus, all Jews were considered to be idolaters and later were attacked by Muhammad's warriors. They were subdued and required to pay taxes for not converting to Islam.[xv]

The Jews also were looking for a sign to prove that he truly was a prophet, but Muhammad could not offer any proof. He could not do a single miracle to provide evidence that he was a prophet.

Thus he tried using the Old Testament as a way of impressing the Jews. However, his knowledge of the Old Testament stories was not accurate. He did not have a personal knowledge of Hebrew Scripture.

For example, the Koran would feature his stories of Moses' confrontation with Pharaoh. In the first 89 chapters he mentions this event 27 times. In other words every 3.3 chapters in the Koran he repeated this story. Yet not one time did he include the most important component of the story—the Passover.

Therefore, how could the Jews accept as their prophet a man who did not know about the Passover nor understood its importance?

The following are other examples:

The Koran states that Adam and Eve did not sin in an earthly garden but sinned in paradise. Muhammad had Adam and Eve cast down to earth after they sinned (*Sura* 7:19-25).

Muhammad taught that Haman, a Persian in the Book of Esther, was an associate of the Pharaoh in Egypt 900 years earlier in the days of Moses (*Sura* 28:8).

Muhammad confused King Saul, mentioned in 1 Samuel, with Gideon, who in Judges 7:1-7 chose 300 warriors out of 10,000 men by observing how they drank water (*Sura* 2:249-250).

How could Muhammad expect the Jews to accept his "revelations" when he taught outright errors about the Old Testament in a city in which numerous Jews knew these stories? He responded to the rejection of the Jews by choosing to purge them.[xvi]

His Constitution of Medina

Soon after Muhammad arrived in Medina in September 622, his first task was to consolidate the various Arab clans and the Jewish tribes into one unified front. By drawing up a new constitution he was remarkably successful in unifying the various factions.[xvii]

This document is known as the Constitution of Medina. This document declared the existence of the community of people (*umma*) who looked to Allah as God and to Muhammad as the prophet of Allah. However, he did not win the support of the Jews.

Muhammad Becomes a Warrior

His followers had little food and clothes. For him to obtain money for his new theocracy was essential. To raid each other was common among Arab tribes of that day. In *Sura* 9:73, which says, "O prophet! Strive hard against the unbelievers and the hypocrites, and be firm against them. Their abode is hell—an evil refuge indeed", Allah gave him permission to rob caravans on their route to Mecca.

He began to send out his raiding parties. These raids kept the new religion functioning and began to shape Islamic theology. No less than 25 of these raids were recorded. Muhammad himself participated in many of them.[xviii]

Ibn Warraq says that "it was during this period Muhammad was no more than the head of a robber community, unwilling to earn an honest living".[xix]

One of the raids was at Nakhla, a settlement not far from Mecca. Muhammad himself was not present, but his raiders attacked the caravan during the sacred month of Rajab. However, fighting was forbidden during this month.

In *Sura* 2:217 Muhammad received a new revelation from Allah. Muhammad justified the raid occurring in the sacred month. It stated that opposing the raid was a more serious transgression than was violating the sacred month of Rajab. Several times throughout the Koran, Allah makes special exceptions from previous laws for Muhammad.

Robert Spencer writes, "This revelation led to an Islamic principle: Good became identified with anything that benefited Muslims regardless of whether it violated moral or other laws. Moral laws and the Ten Commandments were swept aside in favor of the principle of expediency".[xx]

His Break with the Jews

The Jews both rejected and ridiculed Muhammad, so he changed the Koran to say that they no longer were to pray toward Jerusalem but to the Kaaba at Mecca (*Sura* 2:142 and *Sura* 2:125). Some of the Jewish fasts and feasts also were eliminated. He began to accuse the Jews of tampering with their own Scriptures.[xxi]

His Battle of Badr: a Key Battle in Islam

The Koran records a major battle called the Battle of Badr occurring in

March 624. This is a battle in which Muhammad participated. At this time Mohammad realized that the Jews posed a real threat to his slowly increasing power; this battle marked a true turning point.[xxii]

Muhammad heard that a large Quraysh tribe caravan had lots of money and that it was proceeding in their direction from Syria. He told his followers to go and attack it.[xxiii]

Muhammad had 300 men; the Quraysh tribe had nearly 1,000. The two groups met at a place called Badr. The Muslims were outnumbered by more than three to one.[xxiv] In the Koran Muhammad had taught his men that their loyalty to Islam overrode all other human bonds (*Sura* 9:23-24, 59:22-23).

Forty-five men from the Quraysh tribe were killed; this included some of the leading men of Mecca. Seventy-five were taken prisoner. The Muslims lost only 14 people.

The victory at Badr was the turning point for Muslims. Muhammad even claimed that armies of angels joined with the Muslims to smite the Quraysh tribe and that they could expect similar help in the future (*Sura* 3:123-125).

Another revelation to Muhammad from Allah emphasized that the commitment to Allah and not military might brought victory at Badr (*Sura* 3:13).

Sura 8:17 asserts that at Badr the Muslims were only passive instruments.

Chapter 8 of the Koran is entirely devoted to reflections on the battle of Badr. It is titled, "The Spoils of War" or "Booty". At Badr so many spoils of war existed that this created jealousy. This was so divisive that once again Muhammad received a revelation from Allah.

Allah warned the Muslims not to consider the spoils won at Badr to belong to anyone but Muhammad, "the Messenger" (*Sura* 8:1). Some later have found this assertion by Allah extremely convenient for Muhammad.

Muhammad kept one-fifth for himself and distributed the rest of the spoils among the Muslims equally (*Sura* 8:41). Allah said this was Muhammad's reward for being obedient (*Sura* 8:69).

By this battle in 624 Muslims now were a force with whom the pagans of Arabia had to deal. Muslims began to strike terror in the hearts of the people whom they considered their enemies. Muhammad claimed to be the last of the prophets; his victory at Badr was his confirmation.

This battle was followed by many other battles in which Muhammad tried to eliminate the Jews. *Sura* 47:4 says that anyone who opposes Muhammad and his new religion deserves a humiliating death by beheading if possible. "Therefore, when ye meet the Unbelievers (in fight), smite at their necks; at length, when ye have thoroughly subdued them" (*Sura* 47:4).

After he eradicated the Jews at Medina, Muhammad quickly progressed to his final goal: the conquering of Mecca.[xxv]

Muhammad went from being purely a "warner" who called the Quraysh tribe to turn away from idols to the worship of the one true God to becoming a warrior to fight for Allah.

The foundation was being laid not only for the final conquest of Mecca and Arabia but ultimately for the conquest of the whole world, until all were brought into subjection to Allah. This is the goal of Islam.

His Capture of Mecca

In 628 Muhammad and Meccan leaders signed a 10-year peace treaty. This famous treaty is known as "The Treaty of Hudaybiah". The treaty granted Muhammad and his followers permission to make pilgrimages to Mecca. The treaty also stipulated that for the next 10 years both sides would not fight each other.

In 630 the Quraysh tribe in Mecca broke the truce and killed several allies of Muhammad. He was so outraged that he prepared an army of 10,000 men to march on the city of Mecca and to slaughter anyone who resisted.

Muhammad entered the city and was met with little resistance. He went straight to the Kaaba and circled it seven times as he rode on his camel. He then demanded that the door be opened. He entered the sanctuary of the stone, took out a wooden dove idol, and scattered its decaying material on the ground.

He said, "the truth has come and falsehood has passed away". He erased pictures from the walls; these included those depicting Christ and the Virgin Mary; hereby the Kaaba was cleansed of pagan gods.

He stood at the door of the Kaaba and addressed the Meccans who pleaded for mercy. He said, "There is no God but Allah . . . ".[xxvi]

The center of Islam now was firmly established. Muhammad demanded that all Muslims make a pilgrimage to the Kaaba; to this day the Kaaba stone is the focal point of the Islamic faith. Every year millions go to pray around it.[xxvii]

His Final Years and Death

After this event things began to change. Women began wearing veils as the wives of Muhammad did.

He gained the respect of the Meccans. Other tribes joined the *umma* — the community of Islam. He led an army of 30,000 against the tribe of Tabuk. He brought all of Arabia under his control.[xxviii]

Muhammad owned Arabia. Christians and Jews were allowed to practice their own faith, but they had to pay a tax (*Sura* 9:29). It was one of his greatest accomplishments, because by doing this he was able to unify a powerful nation under Islam; to this day it remains so.[xxix]

In February 632 Muhammad made his last pilgrimage to Mecca from

Medina. He went back to his home in Medina and spent his last days with his wife, Aisha. On June 8, 632, at age 63 he died an unexpected and sudden, natural death. He left no sons, he had no heirs, and he had not appointed any successor. He was buried at his home.

Conclusion

Who was Muhammad? Is Muhammad to be followed as the perfect example of obedience to God? That is the big question of religious history? Muslims say "yes"—he was a true prophet of God and the perfect example of moral behavior for mankind.

After Muhammad's death Islam spread rapidly by means of fighting and conquest. Northern Africa, much of which was Christian, was taken by the sword in the name of Islam. These Islamic warriors later moved armies into other parts of the world such as Europe, the Middle East, and Asia. The militant stronghold of Islam over its people was and to this day is very powerful. This important foundational element of Islam creates intense pressure for a person living in an area dominated by an Islamic majority not to convert to any other religion. It makes Islam a religion of fear. All Muslims must ask themselves what the ramifications, not only for themselves but also for their families, would be if they ever were to consider a different faith. Yet the Holy Spirit of God is more powerful than are the armies of people. First John 4:18 says, *But perfect love drives out fear*.

Despite the fear of persecution and death Muslims today are trusting Christ. They are being freed from a wall of darkness set up by one man, Muhammad.

Chapter 2

The Holy Book, The Koran

On a flight to an African nation I had the opportunity to discuss with a Muslim who was seated next to me the subject of Islam.

I asked, "Do you know what your problem is in Islam?"

He responded, "What?"

I said, "You do not have a New Testament which cancels out all of those old laws and violent scriptures." I then explained to him that Jesus fulfilled the law and replaced with love and forgiveness the harsh consequences of the Old Testament law.

What is the Koran? What is in it? What teachings are causing violence around the world?

The Bible says, *In the beginning was the Word . . .. The Word became flesh and made His dwelling among us* (John 1:1, 14). Christians believe that God revealed Himself in the person of Jesus Christ. Jesus Christ is eternal.

In Islam "in the beginning was the Word and the Word became a BOOK". Throughout the Koran we are reminded that it is totally from

Allah himself who is revealing it to the prophet, Muhammad.[xxx]

The Koran is the foundation of the Islam religion. Without an understanding of the Koran, understanding Islam is not possible. The word *Koran* means "reciting". Muslims believe that throughout a period of 23 years the angel Gabriel gave Muhammad the Koran[xxxi] (*Sura* 25:32, 17:106).

For Muslims the Koran is eternal. In other words, from their viewpoint the Koran always has existed and has no beginning. This also is an attribute of God. God is eternal. He has no beginning and will have no end.

Muslims believe that the Koran reveals the full wisdom of Allah. It is true, honorable, glorious, free from error, protected from evil spirits, provides guidance, and is a book that only Allah Himself could produce. Thus it is a holy book to be respected and revered.

Muhammad gave his revelations only orally. While he was alive, he was considered to be the mouthpiece of Allah; he did not see the need to write down his revelations. However, after he died, the need of collecting and compiling this final revelation in written form arose.

Collecting the Koran

In 633 about one year after Muhammad died, the battle of Yamamah occurred. In this battle a large number of Muslims who had memorized the Koran were killed.

The first Caliph (leader) was Abu Bakr. He asked a man by the name of Zaid Ibn Thabit to collect in one book the different fragments of the Koran. Zaid said that he collected it from parchments, leafstalks of date palms, and from the memories of men. He eventually finished his work and produced what we now call the Koran.[xxxii]

The third Caliph, Uthman, sent to every Muslim province one copy of what had been collected and ordered all the other Koran material to be burned.[xxxiii]

Chapters and Verses

The Koran is slightly shorter than the New Testament is. It has 114 chapters called *Suras*. Eighty-six were revealed to Muhammad during the Meccan period. Twenty-five were revealed to Muhammad while he lived in Medina.

The *Suras* are not arranged in chronological order, nor are they in a logical order. Dating accurately some of the *Suras* is difficult.

Therefore some *Suras* at the end of the Koran actually were written at an earlier period of time. Some of the first *Suras* are dated later on.

Each *Sura* also has a title that often is derived from a word or a phrase within the chapter. Examples are "The Cow" and "The Fig", etc. In most cases these titles do not indicate the theme of the chapter.

Each *Sura* is divided into verses which are called *ayat*. Each *Sura* begins with a *bismillah*, which is "In the name of God, Most Gracious, Most Merciful."

Some Western scholars have commonly classified the Koran according to two stages: Meccan and Medinan periods.[xxxiv]

To understand the Koran one has to know that the Koran was written in these two distinctive periods of time: the Meccan period and the Medinan period.

The Meccan Period

During this period of Muhammad's ministry he primarily was a "warner", (*Sura* 87:9). He warned the people about idolatry; his revelations simply called on people to believe in one god, Allah, and that he was the prophet. The verses about peace are found in this section.

He also preached about the Day of Judgment. He graphically described the destiny of hell for all who are lost. He preached about the future of the saved in Paradise.[xxxv]

At the beginning of his ministry Muhammad did not attack the pagan gods of Mecca using violence.

The Medinan Period

Later he was preaching in the city of Medina. There his role as well as his revelations changed. In Medina he became a "warrior"; that is the place in which the reader finds the verses about violence and war.

Muhammad established a "political religion and became the 'beautiful model'". Many verses state that he, along with God, was to be obeyed. This is a key point, because he actually equated himself with God. He and God were to be obeyed (*Suras* 33:21, 4:80, 33:56).

Islamic laws, ethics, and the Islamic judicial system largely were developed during this period.[xxxvi]

One important fact about this period was that Muhammad made a final break with the Jewish and Christian faiths of his time because they both rejected him as a true prophet of God. In his denouncements of both Jews and Christians his revelations became more and more forceful and violent.

Abrogation

The Koran has a doctrine called *abrogation*. Unless one understands this doctrine, the person can become very confused about Islam.

This doctrine states that the later revelations of Muhammad *abrogate* (declare null and void) his earlier ones.[xxxvii] In other words during his preaching in Mecca, which was at the beginning of his ministry, Muhammad could make a pronouncement. Then later after he moved to Medina, he would say something else that would nullify what he said earlier.

The doctrine of *abrogation* confuses the modern reader for the very simple reason that the *Suras* are not in chronological order. Through a simple reading of the Koran a modern reader cannot determine what is the earlier and what is the later revelation. Therefore, a later *Sura* in terms of placement in the Koran actually could be abrogated by a *Sura* that is placed earlier but was written later.

Muhammad would simply say that "Allah revealed it to him"; this way he could change things as he was developing the religion.

For example *Sura* 2:106: "None of our revelations do we abrogate or cause to be forgotten, but we substitute something better or similar: knowest thou not that Allah hath power over all things."

Sura 13:39: "Allah doth blot out or confirm what He pleaseth: with Him is the Mother of the Book."

Sura 47:35 calls for Muslims to be a people of peace.

This verse contradicts 9:5, which is called the Verse of the Sword. When he was asked about this contradiction, Muhammad's cousin, Ibn Abbas, said that 9:5 abrogated 47:35.[xxxviii]

We constantly are told that Islam has nothing to do with violence and global terrorism. The problem is that in the Koran one can find verses of peace as well as violence. Which of these verses should we believe? Which of these verses should a practicing Muslim believe?

One needs to understand that the "peace verses" were written when

Muhammad was preaching in Mecca at the beginning of his ministry. At this point Islam consisted only of a small group of followers.

Later this group moved to Medina and grew stronger. In Medina Muhammad's words became harsh toward infidels, Christians, and Jews because they rejected him as a true prophet of God. He taught violence against unbelievers—toward those who rejected him and his message.

For the terrorist today these violent verses abrogate the peace verses, because the violence verses occurred later in Muhammad's revelation. These later verses are the ones that Osama Bin Laden and other terrorists use to justify their actions of terrorism.

Some modern Muslims try to reform the Koran and put these types of verses into a historical context of its time. Unfortunately these men are in the minority; radical Muslims call them "heretics".

Muslims view the Koran as eternal. It is the final word from God; the words in the Koran are for all people for all time. They can not be changed in any way to mean other than what they meant in Muhammad's time. This presents a difficult problem for the current-day, moderate Muslim.

Another example of abrogation is in *Sura* 2:142 and 2:125.

In *Sura* 2:142 Muhammad ordered Muslims to pray toward Jerusalem. After the Jews of Medina rejected him as a true prophet of God, he became angry with them. He then received another revelation from Allah and ordered Muslims to pray toward Mecca (*Sura* 2:125). Thus *Sura* 2:125 abrogates *Sura* 2:142.

Numerous later verses abrogate earlier verses. This concept of abrogation contradicts the concept that the Koran is eternal and cannot be changed.

Sharia Law: The Key to Understanding Islam

Most Western scholars of Islam agree that the overwhelming vast majority of Muslims abhor terrorism and terrorist acts and do not advocate using the Islamic religion as a basis for these acts.

However, all Muslims should believe in Islamic law, which is called *Sharia law*. What is Sharia law? Sharia is derived directly from the Koran, so all Muslims are obligated to believe in Islamic or Sharia law.

Sharia law is the list of commandments and laws which Muslims believe originate with Allah and are in the Koran. They were revealed to Muhammad and control all details of life: religious, social, political, and governmental.

The objective of Islam is to have everyone in the world governed by Sharia law. For people to understand Islam they must realize that Islam is more than a spiritual belief system.

Sharia law is the key to understanding Islamic ideology, government, economics, and social institutions. Sharia applies Islamic theology to a person's everyday life. Islam teaches that Sharia law expresses the universal will of Allah for humankind.

Muslims have a holy obligation to impose Sharia on all the nations of the world. Therefore, Islam conflicts with the ideals of government and social order of free nations throughout the world.

Sharia law gives a clear insight into Islam's objectives for the world's political and social order. Islam is a complete way of life; Sharia law is not compatible with the ideals of freedom.

For example, in Islam no such thing as separation of church and state exists. Women who commit adultery are to be put under house arrest for the rest of their lives. Many of the Sharia rules are in sharp contrast to the Word of God, especially in its treatment of women, human rights in general, and freedom of religion. Some Islamic-controlled nations have the death penalty for a Muslim who converts to Christianity or any other religion.

The goal of Islam is to implement Sharia law over every nation in the world. Muslims view Allah as sovereign; nothing on earth can compete with Him. Everyone and every nation must submit to Allah's laws; all rebellion against Allah's laws must be eradicated.

The Islamic state is based on the principle that all authority belongs to Allah; every nation must establish a political system (*manhaj*) that expresses Allah's sovereignty by being based on Sharia law. This means that both people and nations totally must submit to Allah's laws.

From this perspective secular states must be rejected and are idolatrous. This clash in Western and Islamic political worldviews is the real issue the political world faces.[xxxix]

The Koran and Jews

Once while I was in Malaysia, I was talking to a Muslim from Saudi Arabia; he immediately asked me what I thought about Jews. He was openly hostile toward Jews. When witnessing to a Muslim one needs to be aware that the person may have a prejudice against Jews. Muslims get this prejudice from the Koran.

Sura 2:63-65 Disobedient Jews will be transformed into pigs.
 Also, in *Suras* 5:59-60, 7:166.
Sura 2:87 They are arrogant.
Sura 2:96 They are the greediest people on earth.
Sura 2:109 They try to wish evil on people and mislead them.
Sura 5:13 Allah has cursed them.
Sura 5:33 They strive to do mischief on earth.
Sura 5:41 They listen to any lie.
Sura 5:78 They are cursed.
Sura 9:29 They must pay a tax for not being a Muslim.

The Koran and Violence

One may wonder why Muslim terrorists commit so much violence. When we read the Koran, we quickly can understand the basis of the violence.

More than 100 verses tell Muslims to fight against and kill infidels, Christians, and Jews. If just one time Jesus Christ had said for His followers to kill Muslims, Christianity in no way would be considered a "religion of peace". Listed are just a few of the verses in the Koran about fighting, killing, and violence.

Chapter 9 is an extended exhortation on warfare against Jews and Christians.

• *Sura* 2:191-193 Fighting is mandatory.
• *Sura* 2:193 Fight until the entire world is conquered by Islam.
• *Sura* 2:216 Fighting is not optional.
• *Sura* 4:95 Fighting is better than staying home.
• Sura 4:100 Those who fight for Allah are guaranteed reward.
• *Sura* 8:12 Fight against the infidels.

The Koran and Groups of People to Fight or Kill

• *Sura* 4:75 Fight those who oppress others.
• *Sura* 4:91 Kill anyone who leaves Islam.
• *Sura* 9:29 Kill Christians and Jews.
• *Sura* 47:4 Fight unbelievers.
• *Sura* 66:9 Fight hypocrites.

The Koran and Women

• *Sura* 2:223 Wives are like a "field" for their husbands.
• *Sura* 2:230 A man can not remarry his previous divorced wife unless she has also married someone else and divorced him.
• *Sura* 2:282 A woman's witness and word is half that of a man.

- *Sura* 4:11 Women get half the inheritance of a man.
- *Sura* 4:34 Women are to be beaten if they disobey their husbands.
- *Sura* 4:43 Touching a woman can make a man ceremonially unclean until he washes before prayer.
- *Sura* 5:6 Touching a woman can make a man unclean.
- *Sura* 24:33 Slaves should not be forced into prostitution unless they are willing to do so.

The Koran and Slavery

Slavery existed before Muhammad; he did include that system into Islam. Islam did condone slavery. By law a slave was regarded as an inferior person. During the period of Islamic empires, thousands of white slaves were imported from Syria and Central Asia. Beautiful young women were brought from Spain, Italy, Egypt, North Africa, and South Arabia.[xl]

- *Sura* 4:25 Men can marry their slaves.
- *Sura* 33:50 Slaves are a prized gift which Allah gives to Muslim men.
- *Sura* 33:52 Men are permitted to have sex with their slaves.

The Koran is believed to be the eternal Word of God; it can not be changed or updated. Thus these views about slavery remain in the Koran and are active today.

Contradictions and Mistakes in the Koran

The Koran has many contradictions and mistakes in it. In *Sura* 4:82 the Koran says, "Do they not consider the Qur'an (with care)? Had it been from other than Allah, they would surely have found therein much discrepancy."

This verse teaches that if the Koran has contradictions or mistakes, then it is not from God. In this book we will mention only a few of them. These contradictions and mistakes prove the Koran is not a book from God.

• Allah's Words

Sura 2:106 says they can be changed. It says, "None of our revelations do We abrogate or cause to be forgotten, but we substitute something better or similar: knowest thou not that Allah hath power over all things?"

Sura 6:115 says that the words of Allah cannot be changed. It says, "The Word of thy Lord doth find its fulfillment in truth and in justice: none can change His words: for He is the one Who heareth and knoweth all."

• Religion

Sura 2:256 "let there be no compulsion in religion".
Sura 2:193 "And fight them on until there is no more tumult or oppression, And there prevail justice and faith in Allah;"

• First Muslim
Sura 7:143 Moses was the first Muslim.
Sura 39:12 Abraham was the first Muslim.

• Noah's Son
Sura 11:42-43 Noah's son was one of those who drowned in the flood.
Sura 21:76 Noah's family was delivered from drowning.

• Mary's Brother

Sura 19:27-28 Calls Mary, the mother of Jesus, Aaron's sister. Aaron, Moses' brother, cannot possibly be Mary's brother.

• Slandering Women

Sura 24:4-5 "And those who launch a charge against chaste women, and produce not four witnesses (to support their allegations)—flog them with eighty stripes; and reject their evidence ever after: for such men are wicked transgressors—Unless they repent thereafter and mend (their conduct); for Allah is oft-forgiving, Most Merciful." In other words forgiveness is provided for.

Sura 24:23-25 No forgiveness is provided for. "Those who slander chaste women, indiscreet but believing, are cursed in this life and in the hereafter: for them is a grievous penalty—".

Which is correct: forgiveness or no forgiveness?

• **Punishment for Adultery**

Sura 4:15 Women are put under house arrest for life. "If any of your women are guilty of lewdness, take the evidence of four (reliable) witnesses from amongst you against them; and if they testify, confine them to houses until death do claim them, or Allah ordain for them some (other) way." *Sura* 4:16 Men go free if they "repent and amend".

Sura 24:2 Women are to be flogged. "The woman and the man guilty of adultery or fornication—flog each of them with a hundred stripes: let not compassion move you in their case . . .."

Which is correct: flogging for both or house arrest for the woman?

The Koran has so many contradictions and mistakes in it that Robert A. Morey has written a book on this subject.

Should non-Muslims be burning Korans? Of course we should NOT be burning Korans. We should be reading and exposing them! We should encourage people to read the Koran and let it simply speak for itself. A reader of the Koran will discover that a man named Muhammad who was a false prophet once lived. He claimed that he received revelations from a false god, Allah. He formed a false religion. He created a belief system that has been violent to all who oppose it and that leads billions to hell because its founder rejected Jesus Christ as the true Lord and Savior of the world.

PART II
THEIR BELIEFS

Chapter 3

Pillars of the Islamic Faith

Islam has five basic pillars of faith. Some people add a sixth one. Being very familiar with all six of these core values of Islam is wise. Most Muslims will be familiar with these beliefs even if they do not know any additional information about their faith.

Declaration of Faith

How does someone become a Muslim? A person simply must make the declaration that "There is no God but Allah and Mohammad is the messenger of God." This declaration is called "the *shahada*". This declaration of faith is a simple formula that all Muslims pronounce. It is the most-often-repeated sentence in Islam and every day during daily prayers is spoken.

Prayer

Obligatory prayers are performed five times a day and represent a direct link between the worshiper and God. This is called "the *salat*". Muslims pray five times a day toward Mecca: dawn, noon, mid-afternoon, sunset, and late evening. These five prescribed prayers contain verses from the Koran and are said in Arabic, the language of the Revelation. Personal supplications, however, can be offered in one's own language and at any time.

Muslims also are obligated to ritually cleanse parts of their body before they pray. A Muslim must cleanse his or her head, face, scalp, ears, nose, hands, arms to the elbows, and feet.

Although worshiping together in a mosque is preferable, a Muslim may pray almost anywhere, such as in fields, offices, factories, and universities.[xli]

A translation of the *Adan* or Call to Prayer is:

God is Great.
God is Great.
God is Great.
God is Great.
I testify that there is none worthy of worship except God.
I testify that there is none worthy of worship except God.
I testify that Muhammad is the messenger of God.
I testify that Muhammad is the messenger of God.
Come to prayer!
Come to prayer!
Come to success!
Come to success!
God is Great!
God is Great!
There is none worthy of worship except Allah.

Almsgiving

An important principle of Islam is that everything belongs to God; therefore wealth is held by human beings in trust. Muslims are expected to give two-and-a-half percent of their income to charity. This can take the form of food, such as feeding beggars. This is called "the *zakat*", which means "to be pure". To give is to purify one's soul.[xlii]

Fasting

Every year in the month of Ramadan all Muslims fast from dawn until sundown. They abstain from food, drink, and sexual relations with their spouses. This is called the *sawm*.

Those who are sick, elderly, or on a journey, and women who are menstruating, pregnant, or nursing are permitted to break the fast and make up an equal number of days later in the year if they are healthy and able. From puberty children begin to fast (and to observe prayers); many start earlier.[xliii]

The reason for the fasting is for both self-purification and self-restraint.[xliv] By cutting oneself from worldly comforts a fasting person focuses on his or her purpose in life by constantly being aware of the presence of God. In *Sura* 2:183 the Koran states, "O ye who believe! Fasting is prescribed to you as it was prescribed to those before you, that you may (learn) self-restraint."

Pilgrimage

Mecca is the holiest site of Islam. During his or her lifetime every Muslim, if both physically and financially able, is expected to travel to Mecca. Each year from every corner of the globe more than two-million people go to Mecca. This is called the *hajj*. The *hajj* improves one's chances for salvation, cleanses the soul, and wipes away sin.[xlv]

The annual *hajj* begins in the 12th month of the Islamic year (which is lunar, not solar, so the *hajj* and Ramadan sometimes fall in summer and sometimes in winter). Pilgrims wear special clothes—simple garments that strip away distinctions of class and culture, so that all stand equal before God.

The rites of the *hajj* include going around the Kaaba seven times. Muslims also re-enact Mohammad's flight to Medina. In what often is thought as a preview of the Day of Judgment, the pilgrims later stand together on the wide plains of Arafat (a large expanse of desert outside Mecca) and join in prayer for God's forgiveness.[xlvi]

The close of the *hajj* is marked by a festival, the *Id al Adha*, which in

Muslim communities everywhere is celebrated with prayers and the exchange of gifts.

The five pillars of Islam define the basic identity of Muslims. Besides these five pillars in any fair treatment of Islam two other core beliefs need to be addressed. These two are *Jihad* and Sharia law or Islamic law.

Jihad—the Holy War

When he tried to take over Kuwait, Saddam Hussein called for a *Jihad* against America because the United States defended the rights of Kuwait. The *Jihad* largely failed but not entirely. The end result was more than 100 terrorist acts that were committed throughout the world plus the massive demonstrations against the West. These demonstrations were held throughout the many Islamic countries.[xlvii]

In the media we hear a lot about *Jihad*. It sometimes is called the sixth pillar of Islam. *Jihad* is a core value of Islam and is one of the root causes of terrorism in our modern world. What is it?

Islam divides the world into two parts: The first is *dar al Islam*, which is the "house of peace". Peace is for those who submit to Islam.[xlviii] Thus when one hears that Islam is a religion of peace, this simply means that one has peace "if" he or she has submitted to Allah.

The second way Muslims view the world is the *dar al harb*, which is the "house of war". These are the people who either are ignorant or disobedient to Allah. They live in a territory of non-submission or war.[xlix] These people need to enter into the "house of peace", even if force is used to accomplish this goal.

Jihad is from the word *jahada*, which means "to exert one's self". When one practices *jihad*, the person is exerting his or her strength, might, and soul in the service of Allah. The individual is "striving or struggling in the way of God".[l]

• Greater *Jihad*

A tradition in Islam says that Muhammad once returned from a battle and declared that he had returned from the "lesser *jihad*" to the "greater *jihad*". He declared that the "greater *jihad*" was a struggle against oneself.

Verses in the Koran support this view. *Sura* 5:16 says, "Wherewith Allah guideth all who seek His good pleasure to ways of peace and safety, and leadeth them out of darkness, by His will, unto the light — guideth them to a path that is straight."

Within Islam also is a form of *jihad* which is a struggle to better the community. Improving education is a good example of this type of *jihad*.

• Lesser *Jihad*

In the Koran are many other texts that support the "lesser *jihad*", which is to launch a war in the name of Allah against his enemies and Islam.[li]

The goal of Islam is to bring all people into submission of Allah, so everyone can live in the "house of peace". *Jihad* is a means of accomplishing this goal. *Sura* 2:244 says, "Then fight in the cause of Allah, and know that Allah heareth and knoweth all things."

The Koran presents *jihad* as violent; Muslims understand that it is a struggle to bring righteousness and peace on earth. The long history of Islam has revealed that *jihad* is war against those considered to be enemies of Islam.[lii]

For Muslims Muhammad is the model example of how to live. *Sura* 33:21 says, "Ye have indeed in the Messenger of Allah a beautiful pattern (of conduct) for any one whose hope is in Allah and the Final Day, and who engages much in the praise of Allah."

He sets the example for all Muslims. If one wants to know the source of violent acts in Islam, the person needs to look no further than to its founder, Muhammad.[liii]

To finance his new religion Muhammad led raids as the cowboys Jesse and Frank James of the old Wild West did. Whatever the Muslims did was justified, since their cause was just. Muslims believe that only by fighting in *jihad* do they receive forgiveness for all their sins.

The Battle of Badr mentioned in *Sura* 3:121-148 of the Koran was the first practical example of what became known as the Islamic doctrine of *Jihad*; it is a doctrine that holds the key to understanding the conflicts of today.[liv]

Not all of his followers were willing to take up the sword. So Allah announced incentives for those who fought in the cause of Allah. *Sura* 3:195 says, "And the Lord hath accepted of them, and answered them: 'never will I suffer to be lost the work of any of you, be he male or female: ye are from, one another.'"

"Those who have left their homes, and were driven out there from, and suffered harm in my cause, and fought and were slain—verily, I will blot out from them their iniquities and admit them into the Gardens with rivers flowing beneath—a reward from the Presence of Allah, and from His Presence is the best of rewards."

Who should they fight? *Sura* 9:29 says, "Fight those who believe not in Allah nor the Last Day . . . ". This command is operative today and will end only when the enemies are "subdued" and pay a tax for protection if they do not submit to Islam. This tax program ties Islam to the state. In other words, not only is Islam theologically a political religion, but the practice of Islam creates a fiscal policy that instates Islam as a political religion.[lv]

Muhammad gave his prescription for victory over his enemies (infidels)—*Sura* 2:216, which says, "Fighting is prescribed upon you, and you dislike it. But it is possible that ye dislike a thing which is good for you, and that ye love a thing which is bad for you. But Allah knoweth, and ye know not."

Verse of the Sword

Sura 9 is an extended exhortation on warfare against infidels. *Sura* 9:5 commonly is called "The Verse of the Sword".

The Verse of the Sword says, "But when the forbidden months are past, then fight and slay the pagans wherever ye find them. And seize them, beleaguer them, and lie in wait for them in every stratagem (of war); But if they repent and establish regular prayers and practice regular charity, then open the way for them: for Allah is oft-forgiving, Most Merciful."

Jihad Verses

The Koran has more than 100 war verses. If Jesus Christ just one time had said for His followers to kill Muslims (which He, of course, didn't say), in no way would Christianity be considered a "religion of peace".

Listed are only a few of these Koran verses about fighting, killing, and violence. If a Christian shares these with a Muslim and the person says, "You are taking these verses out of context", then simply ask the person to please explain the context of these verses. Your listener will not be able to do it, because in the Koran is very little or no context. Each *Sura* is a unit unto itself. They are not in chronological or topical order. The sequence of the *Suras* had no order at all.

Sura 2:191: Kill infidels everywhere you find them. "And slay them wherever ye catch them, and turn them out from where they have turned you out: . . . but fight them not at the Sacred Mosque unless they (first) fight you there; but if they fight you, slay them. Such is the reward of those who suppress faith."

Sura 2:193: Fight until the entire world is conquered by Islam. "And fight them on until there is no more tumult or oppression, and there prevail justice and faith in Allah."

Sura 3:140: "hurt for hurt". "If a wound hath touched you, be sure a similar wound hath touched the others."

Sura 3:169: States that those who die fighting eat at the table of Allah. "Think not of those who are slain in Allah's way as dead. Nay, they live, finding their sustenance in the presence of their Lord;"

Sura 4:76: Fight against the friends of Satan. "Those who believe fight in the cause of Allah, and those who reject faith fight in the cause of evil: so fight ye against the friends of Satan: feeble indeed is the cunning of Satan."

Sura 4:95: Those who fight for Allah are granted a higher status. "Allah hath granted a grade higher to those who strive and fight with their goods and persons than to those who sit (at home). Unto all (in faith)."

Sura 8:39: Fight those who commit idolatry. "Make war on them until idolatry shall cease and God's religion shall reign supreme".

Sura 9:73: Fight the infidels. "O Prophet! Strive hard against the unbelievers and the Hypocrites, and be firm against them. Their abode is Hell—an evil refuge indeed."

Sura 9:123: Fight unbelievers. "O ye who believe! Fight the unbelievers who gird you about . . .. "

Sura 47:4-6: Cut the heads off of infidels. "Therefore, when you meet the unbelievers (in fight), smite at their necks; at length, when ye have thoroughly subdued them, bind a bond firmly (on them); thereafter (is the time for) either generosity or ransom: until the war lays down its burdens. Thus (are ye commanded): but if it had been Allah's will, He could certainly have exacted retribution from them (Himself); but (He lets you fight) in order to test you, some with others. But those who are slain in the way of Allah— He will never let their deeds be lost."

Dr. Braswell, former professor in Tehran, Iran, says, "*Jihad* becomes a method to persuade, coerce, subdue, and tolerate until Islam is established".[lvi] Once a nation is controlled by Islam, a tax is imposed on all non-Muslims (*Sura* 9:29).

Compare Muhammad's life and words to those of Jesus: "*But I tell you, do not resist an evil person. If someone strikes you on the right cheek, turn to him the other also, and if someone wants to sue you and take your tunic, let him have your cloak as well. If someone forces you to go one mile, go with him two miles. Give to the one who asks you, and do not turn away from the one who wants to borrow from you*" (Mt. 5:39-42).

Chapter 4

Six Core Beliefs

Besides the six fundamental beliefs of Muslims all Muslims around the world agree on the following six core beliefs.

Allah

Muslims believe in only ONE God—Allah. He is transcendent, which means he is superior and above all. The Muslim God, Allah, is distant from both His creation and people. He does not express love for humankind.

Angels

Angels are invisible beings who execute the commands of God. They are not superior to humans, because humans are believed to be the highest form of God's creation. Muslims believe that Allah revealed the Koran, the Holy Book for Muslims, through the angel Gabriel.

Muslims also believe that besides angels, other spiritual beings called *jinns* exist. *Jinns* are intelligent beings and can choose right from wrong. Muslim *jinns* and non-Muslim *jinns* exist. The non-Muslim *jinns* fight against righteousness and cause people to follow the wrong way.[lvii]

Prophets

Muslims believe in 124,000 prophets. The Koran mentions by name only 25. Some of them are Adam, Abraham, Moses, and Jesus.

The Koran mentions Jesus 79 times. He seems to have a somewhat higher status than do others except for Muhammad.[lviii]

Muhammad is the final prophet. Muhammad is called "the Seal of Prophets".[lix] Muslims believe that all the teachings of all the prophets before Muhammad were lost or corrupted. To correct all these other teachings Allah had to reveal to Muhammad his truth and final message. His revelations are in the Koran.[lx]

The Koran and Holy Books

Muslims believe that the Old Testament and New Testaments were Holy Books from God. They believe that the Bible has been both corrupted and changed. The Koran was revealed to Muhammad by the angel Gabriel and is the final message of truth for humankind. Muslims believe that just as Allah was uncreated, so the Koran also was uncreated and eternal.[lxi]

Predestination

Muslims believe that everything that happens is because of the will of Allah. Both good and evil are predestined by Allah.[lxii]

Day of Judgment

Muslims believe that on the Day of Judgment Allah will balance on a scale one's good deeds and bad deeds. Muslims who have been good will go to Paradise IF Allah wills it. They are not assured of eternal life even if they have many good deeds. Islam allows for no atonement for sins.

Chapter 5

God—*Allah*

Whether a Christian should refer to God as *Allah* is controversial. We will look at two considerations: one is theological and the other is linguistic.

First, let's look at the theological issue. Is the Islamic God, Allah, the same as our God, Jehovah (also called *Yahweh* and other Hebrew names)?

Here are some questions:

• Do you believe that Jesus died on a cross for our sins? The Koran says, "no".
• Do you believe that Jesus rose from the dead? The Koran says "no".
• Do you believe that Jesus is God? The Koran says "no".
• Do you believe God is a Father? The Koran says "no".
• Do you believe that God is the Holy Spirit? The Koran says "no".

Our God has revealed Himself in three persons: God the Father, God the Son, and God the Holy Spirit. The Islamic god, Allah, in no way can be the same as our God. Our God is the true, living, creator God of the universe who loves us so much that He sent His Son to die on a cross for our sins.

Secondly, we can study the linguistic issue. In English our word for the Creator is *God*. In Portuguese the word for God is *Deus*. In Spanish the word for God is *Dios*. In Swahili the word for God is *Mungo*. In Vietnamese the word for God is *Duc Chua Troi*.

In English, regardless of one's religion, Evangelical Christians, Jews, Buddhists, Mormons, Jehovah Witnesses, atheists, and Hindus all use the word *God*. *God* is the word for the Creator.

Our responsibility as Christians is to interpret who God is in light of Scripture. The issue is not the word *God* but Who He is. Mormons use the word *God* but have a totally different meaning for the word than Evangelical Christians have.

Allah is the Arabic word for *God*. Arabic has no other way to say the word *God* other than using the word *Allah*. Christians in Muslim nations use the word *Allah* in a linguistic sense to refer to God. However, their concept of Allah is not the same as is a Muslim's. Indonesia, for example, has the largest Muslim population in the world; in their hymnbooks and Bibles Indonesian believers use the word *Allah* to refer to God. The word *Allah* is used in all Arabic Bibles and is used by millions of Christians around the world in a linguistic sense but not in the theological sense.

What do Muslims believe about their god, Allah?

Allah is "transcendent". This is a major point and a major difference between Islam and Christianity.

This means that Allah is above his creation. In Islam he is so separate from his creation that he is unknowable. This makes one an "agnostic".

A Muslim can know only Allah's laws but never know Allah in a personal way. An Islam follower cannot have a personal relationship with Creator God.

In contrast the entire basis of the Christian faith is that we can know God. John 17:3 defines eternal life as knowing God. This verse says, *"Now this is eternal life: that they may know you, the only true God, and Jesus Christ, whom you have sent."* Christianity is all based on relationship, but Islam is not. Islam is based on submitting to God's revelation.

A second major point about Islam's belief in Allah is that he is "one". Muslims believe in the Unity of God. The greatest sin one can commit is to associate the nature of God with creation or humanity. To associate a partner or companion with God is called *shirk*. Allah reveals his will (his laws) to humankind but not himself or his nature.[lxiii]

Therefore, when Christians say that Jesus is God, to a Muslim this is considered to be blasphemy. Such a thing is to associate God with humankind. Muslims believe that Christians worship three Gods: God the Father, God the Son, and God the Holy Spirit.

Chapter 6

Jesus—*Isa*

Who is Jesus Christ? This is the most important question in all of life. John 1:1 says, *In the beginning was the Word, and the Word was with God, and the Word was God.* John 1:14 says, *The Word became flesh and made his dwelling among us.* Therefore, Jesus is God! Jesus is the God-Man. Jesus is Lord! Jesus is our Savior! Jesus is Eternal Life! Jesus is the Lamb of God!

Muslims refer to Jesus as *Isa*. Muslims do not believe in the Jesus of the Bible. They believe some truths but not all. Who is their Jesus?

Muslims believe that . . .

Jesus is the son of Mary.

In the Koran this title occurs 23 times and in the Bible only once.

Sura 4:171 says, "O People of the Book! Commit no excuses in your religion: or say of Allah aught but the truth. The Messiah Jesus <u>Son of Mary</u> was (no more than) a Messenger of Allah and His Word, which He bestowed on Mary, And a Spirit proceeding from Him: so believe in Allah and His Messengers, say not 'Trinity' desist."

Jesus was born of a virgin.

Muslims do believe that Mary was a virgin when Jesus was born. *Sura* 3:47 says, "She said, 'O my Lord! How shall I have a son <u>when no man has touched me?</u>'"

Jesus is the Messiah.

Sura 3:45 says, "Behold! The angels said: 'O Mary! Allah gives thee glad tidings of a Word from him: his name will be <u>Christ Jesus</u> (al-Masih, the Messiah) . . ..'"

The word *Messiah* means "the anointed one". However, Muslims do not attach the same meaning to this word that Christians do. They deny that Jesus is God. For Muslims the term *Messiah* is just a personal name.[lxiv]

Jesus is a prophet only.

Sura 19:30 says, "I am indeed a servant of Allah: He has made me revelation and made me <u>a prophet</u>."

Only once in the Koran is Jesus called a *prophet*. Ten times he is called a *messenger* or an *apostle*.[lxv]

Jesus is the Word of God.

Sura 4:171 says, "Jesus is 'a messenger of Allah, and <u>His Word</u>.'"

Muslim scholar al-Ghazali says that this is a title and does not mean Jesus is God but refers only to the fact that Jesus was created in Mary's womb by a divine command.[lxvi]

Jesus is the Spirit of God.

Sura 4:171, "O people of the Book", referring to Jews and Christians and trying to correct their thinking by saying Jesus was "a spirit proceeding from Him (Allah) . . .."

Muslims do not see this as a divine spirit but only as a soul created by Allah.[lxvii] Seven times the Koran uses the word *spirit* in reference to Jesus. He is referred to as the Spirit of Holiness or the Holy Spirit (*Sura* 2:87, 253, 5:110). At other times God breathes His Spirit into Mary as she conceives Jesus (*Sura* 4:171, 19:17, 21:91, 66:12).[lxviii]

Jesus performed miracles.

Sura 3:49 and 5:100 say that Jesus was a healer and raised people from the dead. Muslims do not believe that these miracles prove that Jesus is God. They say that Allah gave Jesus the power to do miracles.[lxix]

Jesus was not the Son of God, nor is He God.

Sura 25:2 says, "He to whom belongs the dominion of the heavens and the earth: no son has He begotten, nor has He a partner in His dominion."

For Jesus to be the Son of God implies that Allah had sexual relations with a female partner (Mary), which resulted in the birth of Jesus. To a Christian this is absurd. No Christian believes this. However, Muslims are taught that this is what we believe. *Sura* 6:101 says, "How can He have a son when He hath no consort?"

Regarding John 3:16 the King James Version says, "*For God so loved the world that he gave his only 'begotten' son . . ..*" The issue is the word *begotten*. One Muslim apologist said, "The Muslim takes exception to the word *begotten*, because begetting is an animal act, belonging to the lower animal functions of sex. How can we attribute such a lowly capacity to God?"[lxx]

Sura 112:3 says, "He begetteth not, Nor is He begotten."

Christians believe that the term *Son of God* is a title that refers to Jesus as being divine and man. *Son* refers to the humanity of Jesus; God refers to His divinity. Jesus is the God-Man. He is "the Word that became flesh". This does not in any way refer to the idea that God had sex with Mary and produced a son.

Jesus was not crucified, nor did He rise from the dead.

Once while Barbara and I were in Jordan, an Arab guide drove us around. At all times he acted kind and gentlemanly. We began to share Christ with him; he said, "I do not believe that Jesus died on a cross. It was Judas who died." At the time I was not aware of Islamic beliefs, so this was a shock to me.

Jews, Hindus, Buddhists, atheists, and all people from all religions do believe that the man Jesus of Nazareth died on a cross outside of Jerusalem in about 33 A.D. They just do not believe that He died for our sins, but they do believe He physically died.

However, Muslims believe that Jesus did not even die physically. They believe that He was switched and that someone else died. They disagree about who the real person that died was. Some, as did our driver, think the person was Judas. Some traditions believe that Allah made Judas look like Jesus and that Jesus was taken into heaven.[lxxi] Some believe Barabas is the one who died. Muslims have among them no uniform agreement as to who died on a cross that day. Christians know that on that day Jesus Christ of Nazareth died for the sins of us all.

Sura 4:157 says, "That they said (in boast), 'We killed Christ Jesus, The son of Mary, The Messenger of Allah'. But they killed him not, Nor crucified him."

Jesus is not a savior from sin.

Sura 39:7 says, "No bearer of burdens can bear the burdens of another."

The Koran commentary says, "No one else can take your burdens or

58

carry your sins. Vicarious atonement would be unjust. You will have to return to Allah in the Hereafter. You will find that He knows all that you did in this life, and its full significance."[lxxii] Muslims say, "How could the punishment of one man be made applicable to all men?"

This verse teaches that Jesus did not die for our sins. He was not a substitute for sin as the Bible claims. The Bible teaches that *the Lord has laid on Him the iniquity of us all* (Isa. 53:6). Second Corinthians 5:21 (NKJV) says, *For He made Him who knew no sin to be sin for us, that we might become the righteousness of God in Him.*

Jesus will return a second time.

Muslims do believe in the second coming of Jesus (*Sura* 43:61). He will slay all who do not accept Islam as the true religion. He will reign for 40 years, then die, and then be buried next to Muhammad in Medina. On the Last Day He then will be resurrected with all other men and women.

Chapter 7

Sin and Salvation

Once when I met with some Islamic scholars in a mosque, they made the point that none of their prophets ever had committed a sin. They also said that Adam was a prophet.

I then asked, "What about Adam? He sinned when he disobeyed God in the Garden of Eden."

They responded, "No, he did not sin; he made a mistake."

Once when Barbara and I were in Tanzania and were riding in a truck, we found several wild lions lying on the side of the road. As I stood up to take a picture, a huge male lion stood up and with a loud voice roared at me. He was wild for sure.

Suppose I had a baby lion as a pet. I would give her milk, play with her, and raise her. Later I would give her meat to eat. Suppose she became my best friend. Then all of a sudden one day for no reason at all she growled and bit my throat and killed me. Why would she do that? A lion always is capable of doing this, because a lion is born with that nature. A lion is born to be wild. This is natural and would be understandable.

So it is with humankind. The nature of every person is to sin. In school no one taught us how to sin. We just grow up and disobey our parents, lie, lust, steal, and have anger, bitterness, jealousy, and pride in our hearts.

We all inherit a sin nature that we received from Adam when he sinned. Adam's sin is called "the original sin"; it was passed on to his children's children and to us and our children of today.

The Bible teaches we are sinners by nature and by choice and that we all are guilty before God and need a Savior.

Muslims deny this. Islam teaches that "original sin" does not exist. It teaches that we are not born with a sin nature. This is the very opposite of what the Bible in Romans 7:15-25 teaches.

Muslims do believe that one can commit sins, but we do so only by our choice and not because of our nature. The greatest of all sins is called *shirk*. *Shirk* is to assign a partner to God. *Sura* 4:116 says, "Allah forgiveth not (the sin of) joining other gods with Him; but He forgiveth whom He pleaseth other sins than this: one who joins other gods with Allah, hath strayed far, far away (from the right)."[lxxiii]

Salvation in Islam is achieved by works. No Muslim will have assurance of salvation and of spending eternity in Paradise. When one's eternal destiny is all based on works, one cannot know for sure where he or she will spend eternity.

Muslims believe that all will be face to face with Allah in the end time and will have to give an account for all their actions. *Sura* 3:185 says that on that day everyone will be paid recompense.

The Muslim god, Allah, then judges people on the scale. The scale is used to balance one's good deeds against his or her bad deeds. Allah will have a "Book of Deeds". He then will make His judgment of whether one will go to heaven or hell.

This is an arbitrary decision of Allah, because Islam teaches predestination. In Arabic it is called *qudar*, which means "destiny". This means that Allah already knows everything and has decreed all happenings in the world according to His will and wisdom.[lxxiv]

Muslims hope that Allah will accept their souls if three things occur:

• One accepts Allah as the only God and Muhammad as a prophet.
• One does good works and obeys the laws that Allah requires of him or her.
• One is predestined by Allah to go to Paradise.[lxxv]

Thus Muslims can believe in Allah and Muhammad and do their best to obey all of the Islamic laws and still not be predestined by Allah to go to Paradise. Until Judgment Day an adherent of Islam cannot know if he or she is part of the "elect".

In contrast to Islam the Bible teaches that we are sinners by nature and choice and that by good works we cannot save ourselves. Salvation is a free gift from God (Eph. 2:8-9). The Bible says only ONE payment for sin exists—only ONE. That payment is death. Romans 6:23 says, *For the wages of sin is death . . ..* The Bible teaches that *while we were still sinners, Christ died for us* (Rom. 5:8). He rose from the dead (Rom. 10:9).

Allah forgives whom he chooses. Jesus forgives all sinners who by faith turn to Him and turn their lives and souls over to Him as Lord and Savior. Romans 10:9 is the clearest verse in the Bible that explains how to be saved. This verse says, *That if you confess with your mouth, "Jesus is Lord" and believe in your heart that God raised him from the dead, you will be saved.* To confess Christ as Lord means to turn one's life over to Jesus' control. That is repentance. To believe in one's heart is true faith.

In Islam one "hopes" he or she can go to heaven. In biblical Christianity *He who has the Son has life* (1 John 5:12).

Chapter 8

Afterlife

In the Koran death and judgment are frequent topics. *Sura* 3:185 says, "Every soul shall have a taste of death: and only on the Day of Judgment shall you be paid your full recompense."

Sura 6:93 says, " . . . at death!—the angels stretch forth their hands, (saying), 'yield up your souls: this day shall ye receive your reward . . . .'"

For an unbeliever death is terrifying. *Sura* 8:50 says, "If thou couldst see, when the angels take the souls of the unbelievers (at death), (How) they smite their faces and their backs, (saying): 'taste the penalty of the blazing fire . . . '".

All believers in Islam must wait for the future resurrection. Between death and resurrection people are in a deep sleep. One will not know whether he or she is going to heaven (paradise) or hell. In Islam one has NO assurance of salvation UNLESS the person has been a martyr for Allah.

Resurrection and Judgment

For Muslims the resurrection and judgment day are the same event. Except for the topic that God is one, the Koran refers to the judgment day more than it does any other subject. Judgment day is described in various ways. It is the *day of wrath*, the *day of decision*, and the *day of truth*.

Muslims believe that Allah will resurrect all who have died. The name of *Sura 75* is *The resurrection*. *Suras 82* and *84* also describe the resurrection. At this time natural disasters will occur. Graves will be opened. The earth will perish.[lxxvi]

On the last day Allah will sound a trumpet. All bodies in the grave will rejoin their souls; all will stand before God to be judged. *Sura* 17:13-14 says, "Every man's fate we have fastened on his own neck: On the Day of Judgement [sic] we shall bring out for him a scroll, which he will see spread open. (It will be said to him) 'Read thine (own) record; sufficient is thy soul this day to make out an account against thee.'"

All will be face to face with Allah and will give an account for all their actions. *Sura* 3:185 says, " . . . only on the Day of Judgement [sic] shall you be paid your full recompense." This means that on that day everyone will be paid his/her recompense.

Allah will judge people on the scale of absolute justice. The scale is used to balance one's good deeds against his or her bad deeds. Allah will open the "Book of Deeds" and make his judgment about whether one will go to heaven or to hell.

If on the scale the good deeds outweigh the bad deeds, then that person will go to paradise, but even this is an arbitrary decision of Allah.

If the evil deeds are heavier, the person will be cast into the fires of hell (*Sura* 23:102-103).

Paradise/Heaven

If a person is male, the Muslim who does get to heaven will enjoy a place of incredible delight. Faithful men are even promised beautiful young women. They will drink wine while they lie down on soft, silken couches

(*Sura* 37:45-47).

The Islamic paradise is the same as what Christians call *heaven*—life after death. The paradise contains such important items as beautiful virgins, young boys, water, wine, fruit, and wealth.

Women and Virgins—Muhammad's Heaven Is a Sensual Place.

Muhammad emphasized to his followers that in paradise they would get untouched virgins. Once his followers go to heaven, they can conveniently exchange their wives for the fresher and more pleasurable sexual encounters with beautiful virgins. *Sura* 37:48-49, "And besides them will be chaste women; restraining their glances, with big eyes (Of wonder and beauty). As if they were (delicate) eggs closely guarded."

Sura 44:51-55 Large-eyed women are in Paradise for Muslim men.

Sura 52:17-20 The righteous will be in gardens, delivered from the penalty of fire. 52:20, "They will recline (with ease) on thrones (of dignity) arranged in ranks; and we shall join them to companions, with beautiful big and lustrous eyes."

Sura 55:56-57 "In them will be (maidens), chaste, restraining their glances, whom no man or Jinn before them has touched—Then which of the favours [sic] of your Lord will ye deny?"

Sura 55:70-77 "In them will be fair (companions), good, beautiful . . .." "Whom no man or Jinn before them has touched—."

Sura 56:35–36 "We have created (their Companions) of special creation, and made them virgin-pure (and undefiled)—."

Youth

Sura 52:24 says, "Round about them will serve, and (devoted) to them,

Youths (handsome) as Pearls well-guarded."

Sura 56:17 says, "Round about them will serve youths of perpetual (freshness)."

Sura says, 76:19 says, "And round about them will (serve) youths of perpetual (freshness): if thou seest [sic] them, thou wouldst think them scattered pearls."

Water and Wine

In the dry deserts of Arabia was a shortage of pure water; wine was an extremely precious commodity. Muhammad promised his followers abundant pure water, rivers, fountains, and wine in paradise. This would have helped to attract some who may appear hesitant to join him as he participated in lethal aggression, looting, and plundering people of other religions to finance his people. (*Sura* 3:136, 198, 13:35, 15:45, 47:15 are just a few verses that make this point about water in heaven.)

Muhammad had a problem with promising wine because Allah had declared intoxicants as sinful. However, the wine that they will drink in paradise will be not cause intoxication (*Sura* 37:40-48, 47:15, 56:7-40, 83:23-26).

Wealth, Cushions, Carpets, Gold, Jewels

Muhammad made sure that his followers would have plenty of worldly things to pursue in heaven (*Sura* 22:23, 43:68-73, 44:51-55, 55:70-77, 56:7-40, 76:13-21).

Hell

On several occasions I have taken my students to an Islamic Center to discuss with the *Imam* (leader) and other Islamic scholars about their religion. One of the opening statements they made to me and my students was, "Islam means to submit to God. One must also believe that Muhammad was a prophet. If not, you will be doomed to hell." This was a very startling opening statement to make to university students.

What is the Islamic hell? The best description of the Islamic hell is in the Koran; it speaks for itself:

Islamic scholars believe that *Sura* 19:71 describes that a bridge crosses over to Hell and that all must walk over it. *Sura* 19:71 says, "Not one of you but will pass over it:" This is also based on a *Hadith* (tradition) 8:5777.[lxxvii]

Yusaf Ali, in his footnote number 2518 in the Koran, says that "every soul must pass through or by or over the Fire . . . some refer this verse to the Bridge over Hell, the Bridge *Sirat* over which all must pass to their final Destiny. This bridge is not mentioned in the Qur'an."[lxxviii]

Sura 15:44 Hell has seven gates.

Sura 74:30-31 Nineteen angels guard the seven gates.

Sura 6:128, 11:105-107, 14:16-17, and 37:33 There will be no escape from hell.

Sura 37:62-67 People will eat from a tree called *Zaqqum* that springs from the bottom of Hell. Its shoots are like the heads of devils. People will eat this and will be given boiling water to drink.

Sura 88:6-7 People will eat a bitter food—the plant *Dari*—which neither nourishes nor satisfies.

Sura 37:68 Everyone will be dragged into blazing fire immediately.

Sura 4:56 says that everyone's skin will be roasted.

Sura 38:57 Everyone will have to taste boiling, dark, and murky fluid.

Sura 78:21-25 All will be served either intensely cold or boiling fluid.

Sura 14:49-50 and 22:19-22 All will be weighed down with burning chains and beaten with iron clubs.

Sura 22:19-22 Everyone will be clothed with garments of fire.

Sura 32:20 All will be forced into the fire each time they try to get away.

A mind-boggling conversation occurs between Hell and Allah. Allah asks, "Hell, are you filled up?" The answer comes back, "Are there any more?" (*Sura* 50:30)

Punishment in Islamic Hell is under angelic supervision, but a striking exemption exists—Muhammad's uncle, Abu Lahab, who happened to be a bitter enemy of Muhammad, gets special treatment.

In five verses of the *Sura* 111, Muhammad paints a vivid scene in which Uncle Abu is to burn for eternity. Uncle Abu did not believe that Muhammad was a prophet of God; according to the Koran he paid the price.

His poor wife, not angels, was forced to supply fagots to keep the fire going for Uncle Abu. The Koran falls just short of creating a special compartment for this unfortunate uncle.

Some Muslims view hell as a kind of Islamic purgatory. They believe that before they are allowed to enter paradise, Muslims will spend some time in hell to pay for their sins.[lxxix] Yet, if hell is a purgatory for Muslims, then at some point in the future they will be rescued. This would contradict how *Sura* 6:128 describes hell: "The fire be your dwelling place; you will dwell therein forever."

One thing is for certain. The Islamic hell is for all who reject both Islam and Muhammad as a true prophet of God.

PART III

THE STUMBLING BLOCKS

Chapter 9

Stumbling Blocks

Please understand: in no way can someone reason a person into believing in Christ. One must trust Him by faith. Faith comes by hearing the Word of God.

So, a Christian must use the Word of God when he or she witnesses to a Muslim and must trust the Holy Spirit to convict that person of sin, righteousness, and judgment and lead him or her to Christ (John 16:8).

In my personal experience in sharing Christ with Muslims several stumbling blocks always seem to prohibit them from seeing the light.

We will address some of the most common issues and how in a loving and biblical way to deal with each one. Again, reasoning will not convince a Muslim, but sharing faith in Christ in such a way that helps a lost person clear up his or her doubts and questions is important.

Stumbling Block #1: Who Is Muhammad?

If a Christian witnesses to Muslims enough, before long the Christian will be asked this question, "What do you think or believe about Muhammad?" This is a very sensitive topic. If a Christian says anything negative about Muhammad, Muslims will get highly offended. This question has the potential to become very explosive.

Personally, I never refer to Muhammad as a prophet. I do not believe he was a prophet from the true Living, Creator God. Neither do I respond by saying that I believe he was a false prophet, even though that is what I really believe. A Christian never will win a convert by saying negative and offensive things about someone Muslims admire or revere.

Simply respond by saying, "I know that you believe that Muhammad was a prophet. Let me ask you a question: Who do you believe Jesus Christ was?" By doing this I have not answered his question directly; I also have changed the subject to Christ.

If the person to whom I am talking keeps pressing me about my thoughts on Muhammad, I will honestly say, "I do not believe he was a prophet. If I did, I would be a Muslim. However, I realize that you do revere him to be a prophet; I respect that."

Then I will just note that in *Sura* 46:9, Muhammad says that he did not know for sure that he was going to Paradise (heaven) after he died. This verse says, "I am no bringer of new-fangled doctrine among the messengers, nor do I know what will be done with me or with you."

Muslims do believe that Jesus was a prophet. Thus, a Christian can share that Jesus knows the way to heaven. In John 14:2 Jesus says, "*I am going there to prepare a place for you.*" In John 14:6 Jesus says, "*I am the way and the truth and the life.*" Just simply say, "If you want to know for sure you will go to heaven after you die, then let us study what Jesus says, because he says that He knows the way." In other words "get to the Word; get to Jesus".

Answering this question properly can be a golden opportunity for one to turn the entire conversation to Christ.

Stumbling Block #2: The Bible

One afternoon while I was in Mwanza, Tanzania, I went to the local ice-cream shop in the center of the city. This occurred during Ramadan, so the shop was closed during the daytime, but the owner was sitting out on the sidewalk. Ramadan is the month-long fast that Muslims observe each year to remember when Muhammad received his first vision. Thus we began a very polite conversation. This was easy to do, since this was his holy month.

I simply asked him to explain to me the meaning and the rules of Ramadan. By doing this I was showing interest in his faith. I just listened to him for a while as he explained its purpose and how he personally was observing the holy month. This is a time in which Muslims do not eat or drink during the daytime, but they do at night. In practice they flip-flop the eating times.

I then asked him whether I could explain my faith to him. He immediately responded that our Bible had been changed and corrupted. I told him that I understood that he believes that, but then we continued our polite conversation. After spending quite some time sharing with him about this subject, he responded by saying, "I have learned some new things I have never heard before."

How do you answer the statement almost all Muslims will make, "The Bible has been changed and corrupted"?

Explain several things about the Bible:

During his entire life Muhammad believed that the Bible was the Word of God and had not been changed. *Sura* 6:115 says, "The Word of thy Lord doth find its fulfillment [sic] in truth and in justice: none can change His Words: for He is the one who heareth and knoweth all."

No adequate response to this exists, because in this *Sura* the Koran itself is saying that the Bible is the Word of the Lord and can not be changed.[lxxx]

Point out that if the Bible was changed before or during Muhammad's day, then the Koran is not true, because this verse says the Bible IS the Word of God and has NOT been changed.

The Koran, in *Sura* 10:94, says that if one has any doubts about the faith, to go to the Bible. That *Sura* says, "If thou wert in doubt as to what We have revealed unto thee, then ask those who have been reading the Book from before thee: the Truth hath indeed come to thee from thy Lord: so be in nowise of those in doubt."

The Law and the Gospels of the Bible, which we have today, are the same as the Bible that existed during Muhammad's day. These originals have not been changed.

According to the Koran, during Muhammad's day the Bible had not been changed or corrupted. Later Muslim scholars learned that the Bible contradicted the Koran. They were in a serious dilemma.

They created "a myth" that the Bible had been changed and corrupted. They have NO evidence. If it had been changed, then it had to have been changed AFTER Muhammad's time, or else the Koran would be wrong.

A theory was created that the Bible was changed AFTER Muhammad had died. However, a serious problem exists with this theory. The Old Testament originally was written in Hebrew. The New Testament was written in Greek. These were in existence when Muhammad lived; they exist today. So, how could they be changed?

Also, by the time of Muhammad, the Bible already had been translated in many different languages throughout the known world. All of them said the same thing because they all were based on the original Hebrew and Greek Bible that was in existence during Muhammad's lifetime. Every version in the world, whether they be Russian, English, Chinese, Spanish, Portuguese, French, Arabic, etc., all are based on the Hebrew and Greek versions.

In light of this, what proof do Muslims have that these originals were changed when the Koran itself said they were not?

If the Bible was changed AFTER Muhammad's time, then a "big" question has to be answered. How could the Bible possibly be changed or corrupted, since it was already in many languages all over the world? How could someone possibly collect them all up and change them all?

Consider this illustration: Let's say I wrote a book in English today, Then 570 years later someone happens along and says that my book is an original and a very good book.

My book also is translated into 100 different languages throughout the world. All of them say the same thing. These translations are good and perfect copies of my book.

Later someone arises who says that my original book was changed. Yet, when the reader looks at the earliest copies of my book, they all are the same and the translations of my book are the same.

What proof exists that my book was changed? The copies we have today are the same as the original ones. So, who changed it? When and how could that be done?

For my book to be changed someone would have to collect every version from every language in the entire world and change them all and even collect the original one. That would be impossible.

Muslims throughout the world are taught that our Bible has been changed and corrupted from the original versions. When one begins sharing with a Muslim, statements about the Bible's being changed and corrupted are very normal and typical.

At this point begin focusing on the character of God. Simply point out that the Koran itself says the Bible is truth and that nothing can change

God's words (*Sura* 6:115).

Ask the following questions:

• Do you believe what the Koran in *Sura* 6:115 says about the Bible?
• Do you believe that God is all powerful and is powerful enough to protect His own Word?
• Do you really believe that God will allow someone on earth to change His Word?
• How did the Bible get changed?
• When was it changed?
• Who changed it?

Share that your God is so powerful that He will protect what He said as truth and that no one can change it. Even the Koran teaches this. Believing that it was changed is more difficult than is believing that it never was changed. The truth is that the original Hebrew and Greek Bible that we have today has never been changed from the time they were written. Even the Koran says it can not be changed.

Stumbling Block #3: The Trinity and Deity of Christ

While I waited in the Nairobi, Kenya, airport, to catch an airplane, some young men from Saudi Arabia sat down in front of my wife and me. Thus we began a conversation about our faith.

One of the young men asked, "Do you believe that Jesus is God?"

"Yes", I responded.

"Do you believe that Jesus Christ died on a cross?"

"Yes, I do."

"Then are you telling me that God died?"

He stated the issue about as well as anyone I have ever talked to. Islam regards as blasphemy the Christian concept of the Trinity. They accuse Christians of believing in three gods: God the Father, God the Son, and God the Holy Spirit.

Muslims accuse Christians of idolatry. At some point anyone talking to Muslims will hear this accusation.

In Islam the greatest sin above all sins is called *shirk*. This is when one equates or associates anyone or anything to the Muslim god, Allah. Thus, when a Christian says that Jesus is God, in the eyes of a Muslim the Christian has committed blasphemy. For this reason Christians are considered to be idolaters.

In several places such as *Sura* 6:101 the Koran teaches that God has "no son". Muslims are taught that we, as Christians, believe that God had sex with Mary and that she conceived a son, Jesus. This is not what the Bible teaches; Christians do not believe this. A person sharing his or her faith with a Muslim needs to clearly state this. Muslims have been misled about what we believe about the birth of Christ.

Here is a vital point in sharing Christ: one NEVER can reason a person into the faith. For one to become convinced of this truth or any other truth it will take a miraculous work of the Holy Spirit. Only God Himself can illuminate a heart to the truth of who Jesus is. We do this by sharing the Word of God, which is the Sword of the Lord. He will use His Word to both convince him or her of truth and to convict the person of sin and the person's need of Christ (John 16.8).

Share with the person that the Bible teaches that Mary was conceived by the Holy Spirit and that no sex act was involved. In 3:47 the Koran also teaches that Jesus was born of a virgin, so Muslims will not have a problem with the virgin birth of Christ. "She said, 'O my Lord! How shall I have a son when no man hath touched me?'"

Explain that the term *Son of God* does not mean that Jesus is God's boy. Make it clear that the term *Son of God* is a title.

The word *Son* refers to His humanity. The word *God* refers to His deity. Show the individual the verses found in John 1:1 and 1:14. *In the beginning was the Word, and the Word was with God, and the Word was God"* and *The Word became flesh and made his dwelling among us.*

I simply say, "God is a big God. He is so big that I do not claim to understand all about Him. If I did, He would be too small. Some things about God we accept by faith. So, since He is God, He can do whatever He wants to do; He has the power to do it. For God to become a man is no problem. He can be God-Man if He wants to be. My finite mind does not understand it, but I do accept this by faith, because His Word tells me this is what God did and who Jesus is."

Stumbling Block #4: The Death of Christ

Jews, Hindus, Buddhists, atheists, and agonistics all believe that a man named Jesus of Nazareth died on a cross outside Jerusalem in 33 A.D. They just do not believe that Jesus died for their sins.

Muslims do not believe that Jesus even died on a cross at all (*Sura* 4:157). They believe that He was switched at the last moment and that someone else died instead of Jesus. They disagree who that person was. Some think it was Judas. This is a complete denial of history. Even secular historians never questioned then or now that a Jesus of Nazareth who was crucified outside of Jerusalem that day actually existed.

This is taught only in the Islamic religion. Muslims are taught this from birth because they do not believe any true prophet of God can suffer a death of this nature.

How does one deal with this stumbling block? Only one way exists. Show what the Word of God says. No one will ever win an argument about this. God Himself must convince them of truth by means of the Holy Spirit.

Again, even if someone says that he or she does not believe the Bible, a person sharing his faith in Christ must share the truth from the Word of God. Simply acknowledge that you understand that the individual does not accept the Bible as the Word of God but that you are just showing the person what Christians believe. God will use His Word to convince someone of truth. Remember, the Word of God is the Sword of the Lord.

Once while I was at the Islamic Center in Jackson, TN, I was having a dialogue with the *Imam* (their spiritual leader) and several other faithful Muslim followers. They were making a point about prophets and said that none of the prophets—not just Jesus—had ever sinned.

I then asked about Adam, because Muslims do believe that Adam was a prophet. I mentioned to them that in the Garden of Eden, Adam disobeyed God. Their answer: "Adam did not sin; he just made a mistake."

If someone does not have a biblical understanding of sin, then that person never will see the need to believe that Christ died on a cross. Thus, the first important thing is to teach what the Bible says about sin, its consequences, and the atonement of Christ. In chapter 15, "Sharing the Gospel", you can read more about this as you read in-depth Bible studies about "sin" and also "The Atonement".

PART IV
SHARING YOUR FAITH

Chapter 10

Two Keys

As you consider evangelizing Muslims, you can view this ministry much like the work of Jesus and Paul in New Testament times. When Jesus was born, the government was ruled by the Romans. However, they allowed the Jews to control much of their governmental affairs and especially their religious issues.

Their religious leaders were legalistic. They were the Pharisees and the Sadducees. Their source of authority was the first five books of the Bible. These were called *The Torah* and gave Jewish laws about every aspect of life. This is similar to the Koran and today's Muslim laws called *Sharia law*.

However, besides the law were traditions. People were expected to obey both the law of Moses and the traditions of people. Muslims have the Koran, but they also have their traditions called the *Hadith*.

During New Testament times society was highly male-dominated. So, too, is the Muslim society of today. Under Jewish tradition during the time of Jesus the way to get to the Kingdom of God was by obeying the law—in other words, salvation by works. Muslims believe this exact same way.

When Jesus arrived on the scene, He was rejected. Muslims reject

Jesus today as being Lord and Savior.

Jesus was rejected because He claimed to be God. The leaders accused Him of blasphemy because of His claim. He forgave people of their sins; only one—God—can forgive sin. Jesus preformed miracles to demonstrate His divinity.

He was God-Man. Philippians 2:6-8 says that Jesus was in the form of God and was equal with God. John 1:14 says, *The Word became flesh and made his dwelling among us*. Jesus is God; when He proclaimed this truth, the leaders wanted to kill him. The deity of Christ also is one of the major issues with Muslims today.

People rejected Jesus because He broke the religious traditions of His day and community (Mark 3:1-6). John 1:11 says that Jesus *came to that which was His own, but His own did not receive him*. The religious leaders of His day were hostile to Jesus and finally killed him.

Saul entered the scene; he was the Osama bin Laden of his day. Saul was a terrorist who killed believers in Christ and who wanted to destroy the church. On the road to Damascus when Saul met Jesus, he was miraculously converted. His life was changed; he changed his name to Paul.

When Paul began preaching, even the Christians were afraid of him. Barnabas introduced him to the Christian leaders. He eventually became, outside of Jesus Christ, the greatest missionary who ever lived.

During his missionary journeys Paul constantly faced persecution and suffering. He confronted the traditional teachers of his day.

Paul stated that he had been beaten, imprisoned, experienced riots, sleepless nights, hunger, hard work, hardships, distress, and many troubles and yet was not killed—all for the glory of God (2 Cor. 6:3-10).

Both Jesus and Paul faced very hostile situations. What Jesus and the Apostle Paul experienced also compares with the Muslim world today.

Yet in the midst of that environment the church was started. The church grew. The church multiplied. How did that happen?

Jesus tells us what to do and how to do it. He says, "*go and make disciples*". Disciples are those who have received Christ as Lord and Savior and are students and followers of Jesus. Jesus began with 12. These grew to 120 and then later, by the end of the Book of Acts, to multiple thousands of believers.

The secret of global evangelism lies in two keys which absolutely are essential in sharing with Muslims. I want to address these two keys. I cannot even begin to express adequately the importance of these two keys, because without them one will not bear any fruit in his or her efforts to convert Muslims.

Key #1

The first key is the Holy Spirit of God. To many readers this may sound trite, because this concept seems so obvious. However, I cannot express enough the importance of knowing Who the Holy Spirit is and knowing His work.

The Bible teaches that the Holy Spirit is not a "thing" nor an object. He is a person.

In Hebrews 9:14 the Bible teaches that He is eternal. That means He had no beginning and will have no end.

Psalm 139:7-10 teaches that He is all-present. I can be on the southern costal tip of South Africa and someone else can be in New York City; at the same time the same Holy Spirit will be with both of us.

Luke 1:35 declares that He is all-powerful. In the Bible the word for *power* is the word in which we get our word *dynamite*. No person, president, prime minister, or king on earth has power that can even approach the power of the Holy Spirit.

John 14:26 teaches us that He is all-knowing. No person has any secrets in his or her life and heart that He does not already know.

So, as one studies these verses and many others in the Word of God, one grows to understand that only one person is Eternal, All-Present, All-Knowing, and All Powerful. That is God. So, who is the Holy Spirit? He is God.

Many Christians often use the phrase, "Jesus came into my heart." What does this mean? Do you believe that Jesus died for your sins? Do you believe that He was buried? Do you believe that he rose from the dead? Do you believe that He now is at the right hand of God interceding for you? If you answer *yes* to these questions, then answer this one. How can Jesus be at the right hand of the Father on His throne and be in your heart at the same time? The answer is by means of the Holy Spirit.

The Holy Spirit actually is the One that enters into your heart and life when you give your life to Jesus as Lord and Savior. He lives and dwells in you. First Corinthians 12:13 says, *For we were all baptized by one Spirit into one body—whether Jews or Greeks, slave or free—and we were all given the one Spirit to drink.* That refers to every believer regardless of the person's ethnic group, race, or denomination. If you have received Christ as your Lord and Savior, the Holy Spirit lives and dwells in you.

What is His work? What does He do? He does many things in your life. But our focus in this book is to share that He does several things in the lives of nonbelievers; that includes Muslims.

John 15:26-27 teaches that He is the one who testifies that Jesus is the Truth. How can a person who is taught from birth that Jesus is only a prophet and not the Savior from sin and hell become convinced that Jesus is God, Lord, and Savior? It never will happen unless the Holy Spirit is at work in the heart of that nonbeliever. You will not win a Muslim to Christ through debate, arguments, or reason. It never will happen that way.

John 16:8-11 shares that the Holy Spirit is the one that convicts a nonbeliever of sin, righteousness, and judgment. This is so crucial because a Muslim does not have the same concept of sin as a Christian does. This affects the Muslim's understanding of how to become right with God. This in turns affects his belief in what will happen on judgment day. Who has the ability to totally change his beliefs so he will understand the Biblical view of sin, righteousness, and judgment? Only one person can do that; that person is not you or me but only the Holy Spirit of God.

Key #2

When I was preaching in Virginia, I met a beautiful young woman named Susan (not her real name). She was reared in a very strong and dedicated Muslim family. Her father and mother said their prayers at least five times per day. She was not allowed much of a social life outside her home. She was well-protected. She was taught that she could eat with Jewish persons but not sleep at their house, for they might kill her. She could sleep at Christians' homes but not eat with them for fear they would give her pork. Even though all of her entire life she had heard about Muhammad and Islam, she had her doubts about her religion.

When she went to the university, she had a roommate that was Catholic; thus Susan, for the first time in her life, attended a Christian worship service. However, she did not understand anything going on in that service, so it had no meaning to her. She said, "They all drank from the same cup; that was weird to me." She tried searching for God in many ways and studied various religions. She was a seeker.

She met a young man who was a Christian and who took her to a Bible-believing Evangelical church. Pastor Dan gave her a Bible. It was an entire Bible and one written in modern English. She began reading the Gospel of John. One day she read in Ephesians 4:31-32, *Get rid of all bitterness, rage and anger, brawling and slander, along with every form of malice. Be kind and compassionate to one another, forgiving each other, just as in Christ God forgave you.*

When she read this, these were her thoughts: "God forgave me. That was a foreign concept. My concept was that God has a scale, and He weighs my sin on it. So, I did good things because I had to do them, not because I wanted to. I would get points in my favor by doing good."

She began attending church; six months after God illuminated that verse in her life, she was baptized. She does not know the exact moment when she crossed the line, but it was between the time God spoke to her life through the Word of God and her baptism. Her baptism truly was a public profession of her faith. She did not tell her family but told only about six friends at the university. Her friends, some atheists, attended her baptism because they saw such a change in her life.

She said, "When I was baptized, it felt like a light shining everywhere. I was excited. I had a pure passion about Christ and a complete joy that has never left me."

What was the key to her conversion? It was the Word of God. "The Holy Spirit took the Word of God and applied it to my life," she said.

The second key is the Word of God. God's word is truth. The truth will set each of us free. For a person sharing about Christ, using God's Word when one shares with a Muslim is essential. One may say, "Well, he does not believe in the Bible, so how can you use it in witnessing to a Muslim?"

Once while I shared with a Muslim young man, he said he did not believe the Bible. I simply responded by saying, "Yes, I understand that you do not believe it to be God's Word, but let me show you what it says."

I did not ask him to accept the Bible as truth but simply asked whether I could show him what he was rejecting. In that case he answered, "Yes"; that began a wonderful time of discussion.

The Bible is the "Sword of the Lord". It will prick the heart of an unbeliever; God's Spirit will use the Word to convince him of truth. When the Apostle Paul was in Thessalonica (Acts 17), his approach was to go to the synagogue each Sabbath day. He went there for three Sabbath days and *he reasoned with them from the Scriptures*. That is the key.

What was the result? The Bible says, *Some of the Jews were persuaded and joined Paul and Silas, as did a large number of God-fearing Greeks and not a few prominent women*. In other words many were saved.

This did not occur as a result of Paul using his intellect. It happened because the Holy Spirit of God used the Word of God to convince the nonbelievers of Thessalonica the truth about Jesus Christ.

As you share with Muslims, have faith in these two keys: the Holy Spirit and the Word of God. Be totally convinced with all your heart, mind, and soul that as you use the Word of God, God will use His Spirit to do a work inside their lives.

Chapter 11

Practical Tips

Muslims now live in every part of the globe—both in small-town America as well as major metropolitan cities of the world. They work beside us in our workplaces, sit beside us in our schools, and live beside us in our neighborhoods. We can be sure of one thing: They will carry the Islamic religion with them. We need to be well-informed so we can relate to them, open doors for witness, and be hospitable.

Greetings

Normally a Muslim may ask you about your health or about your family. When a Muslim greets another Muslim, the greeter will say, "Peace be on you." However, if the person says that to you, then you should respond by saying, "And on you be peace."

Shaking Hands

Some of us have to learn things by going through difficult situations. Once while I shared in a Muslim community of Memphis, TN, a car drove up with some women from Somalia. With a smile I greeted them and held out my hand to shake one woman's hand. She did shake my hand but not before she covered her hand so my flesh would not touch hers. At the time I was unaware of *Sura* 5:6 which says that touching a woman will make a man unclean.

Thus, men greeting women can be somewhat awkward if a person does not know the culture well. Many Muslim women will not touch a male's flesh unless it is that of her husband. So, I never again would reach my hand out to shake a woman's hand. If she wants to shake my hand, I would wait and let her reach her hand out first.

For a man things are different. I would stretch my hand out to shake his hand, but it must be my right hand. Muslims consider the left hand the dirty hand. In Third-World countries in which people do not use toilet tissue, the left hand is used for "unclean" functions. Muslims also believe that Satan uses his left hand.[lxxxi]

Refreshments

When a guest is invited into the home of a Muslim, the guest may be invited to partake of some kind of refreshment such as coffee, tea, juice, or cola and something to eat such as nuts or fruit. Also, if you host a Muslim in your home, be sure to offer the Muslim a refreshment (but do not offer pork; see below.)

Gifts

If someone is visiting the home of a Muslim for the first time, the person may want to take a gift. This should be something inexpensive and small such as candy or flowers.[lxxxii] In Eastern culture hospitality and generosity are the two most valued attributes.[lxxxiii]

Food and Drinks

A young Muslim convert once told me that all her life her father told her, "You can play with Jews all day, but do not sleep at their homes, for they may kill you. You can sleep in the homes of Christians, but you cannot eat at their houses, for they may serve you pork." The young woman grew up having both of those fears.

Once while I witnessed to a Muslim young man in Uganda, he asked me just one question, "Do you eat pork?" Pork is the one meat a person never can serve nor offer to a Muslim. A Muslim considers a pig unclean. Muslims do not partake, at least in public, of alcoholic drinks.

Dogs and Camels

Dogs are considered to be dirty animals. They believe that Satan once appeared as a black dog. If someone has a dog and a Muslim visits the person, I suggest that during the visit, the host keep the dog outside. If the dog touches the Muslim, the Muslim will be considered unclean and cannot pray again until the person performs ritual cleansing.[lxxxiv]

On the other hand, a camel is used for transportation and is mentioned in the Koran as an example of wisdom and kindness.[lxxxv]

Politics

At the time of this writing I have been a missionary for more then 40 years. My long-standing policy has been not to discuss politics with people I am trying to reach for Christ. Discussing political matters will not change people's minds, will resolve nothing, and only can be used of Satan to destroy a faithful witness of Jesus Christ. When political issues arise in conversation and I am asked about them, I simply say, "I am not a representative of the United States of America. I am an ambassador of the King of Kings and Lord of Lords—Jesus Christ."

Debates

No one ever has become a Christian by reason. Conversion only occurs as a work of the Holy Spirit. Doubts and questions will arise; wisely answer these questions but never argue with a Muslim about faith in Christ nor about his or her faith. Knowing the basics of the Christian faith and also knowing how to respond to the questions that

Muslims will have such as, "What do you believe about Muhammad?", is important. (One of the purposes of this book is to prepare you to answer these types of questions without getting into an argument or debate.)

Avoid Certain Words

Personally, when I talk to a Muslim, I do not use the word *Christian*. I prefer the term *follower of Christ*. In many parts of the world the word *Christian* has political overtones. For most people it does not have the same biblical meaning as it does for Christian believers.

Also I prefer not using the word *crusade*. If I were inviting a Muslim to attend an evangelistic meeting, I would not use the word *crusade*. This word refers to the Crusades against them. In their minds it is a "war word."

Church

To a Muslim a Christian church service may be very strange. Muslims walk in and see men and women sitting beside each other. In mosques this does not occur. Muslim visitors see people walking around with shoes on. In the mosque shoes are taken off before the person enters. Bibles are left around on pews. This would be strange for a Muslim, who never would do that with the Muslim Holy Book. These are just a few examples of how cultural worship differences between the two faiths occur. Do feel free to invite a Muslim seeker to worship service; beforehand you might wisely share what to expect.

Security

In some parts of the world Muslim evangelism can be very dangerous. Every week somewhere in the world Christians are killed or are persecuted. Be cautious never to reveal the names of Muslim believers. Also never write in a computer, notebook, or even something as personal as a journal or Bible-study prayer notebook the actual names of people who are seeking Christianity. Those persons could be killed. Personally, even in the United States, I do not reveal in a written form the names of Muslim converts. Because of "honor killings" I use false names. I let Muslims themselves reveal whatever information they would like to say about themselves, but I will not do it for the person.

Chapter 12

Person of Peace

Once while I was in India to teach church-planting, I asked this question, "When you go into a new village to start a church, what is the first thing you do?" One man answered with lots of emotion and enthusiasm, "Preach the gospel!" I responded by saying, "Read Luke 10:5 and note what Jesus said to do first."

The term *man of peace* in this context is a man who does not have the peace of God in his heart. He is a seeker. He is not a believer. He is a person in whom the Holy Spirit is working and is preparing him to hear the gospel.

Thus, I shared with the group that the first thing a person who is seeking to share Christ should do is "look for a man of peace". The Bible is filled with examples of "men of peace". Nicodemus in John 3 arrived at night seeking Jesus. Zacchaeus climbed up the sycamore-fig tree and wanted to see Jesus (Luke 19:1-10).

To do effective evangelism a person must have a total and complete confidence in the Holy Spirit. The person must believe the Holy Spirit is at work in the hearts of lost people. The person must believe that the Holy Spirit is doing His job, which is to prepare hearts to hear the gospel.

God is at work all over the world. No place on earth exists in which the Holy Spirit does not live and work. I have a good friend named Sammy Tippet. He once felt led by the Holy Spirit to go to Russia during the Cold War when Communism ruled by force. He went there by faith and had no idea what he would do. God led him to go to a university; he sat down and began to eat his lunch in front of a young man. The young man shared with Sammy that he was reared to be an atheist but that very morning had prayed that if God existed, then for that God to reveal Himself to him. That very afternoon Sammy showed up.

The truth is that God is at work in our world in the hearts of atheists, Buddhists, Jews, Hindus, ancestor-worshipers, and Muslims. People everywhere are searching for peace.

How does someone find a person of peace or a person who is seeking after God? This is easier than one might expect. A follower of Christ can just begin a conversation with a person God has put in his or her life. Ask about the person's life, family, and interests. Then ask the following four questions:

• May I ask you a spiritual question?
• What do you believe about God?
• Would you like to know God personally?
• May I share a story with you about God?

If he says "yes" to the final question, this "may" be a person of peace. If this is the case, making this person a priority in your life is important. Share with the individual a series of Bible studies. I suggest using the stories, The Good News of Jesus, that you will find in the appendix of this book.

All over the entire world my wife, Barbara, and I are teaching this concept. We now have been in more than 60 different nations. We work and minister in some very strong Islamic areas of the world. We train pastors and laypeople to ask these questions; in every place we have been and sent them out the door to go find a person of peace, they have done so without fail. We enter the homes of people of peace and teach them about Jesus Christ. Muslims have opened up their homes for prayer and Bible study. In highly dangerous areas these Bible studies must be done in secret because of the Muslims' fear of being killed. We always want to be sensitive to the situation.

By using visions and dreams God also prepares the hearts of Muslims. Barbara and I were in one nation in which the majority of the population is Muslim. An agriculture missionary worked among them. She and I taught a seminar on making disciples. We met in the top floor of a barn at night. The room was packed; the missionary pointed out a couple on the back row. He said, "They are the only known Christian believers in their people group in the history of the world."

The man was a failure in life and had a very low self-esteem. He wanted to commit suicide. So to end his life, he walked into the forest with poison to drink; his wife allowed him to do so. Before he drank the poison, God gave him a vision. In his mind the man saw that missionary farmer. At night he knocked on the missionary's door and told him his story. Using the stories of both the Old and New Testaments our missionary spent weeks teaching the man the Word of God. The Holy Spirit was preparing the Muslim man's heart to really understand the need of a Savior who died on a cross and who shed his blood for the forgiveness of his sins. He was taught that Jesus rose from the dead and wanted to live in his heart.

The man trusted Christ and secretly was baptized. He told no one he had become a believer in Christ. Had he done so, he could have been killed immediately. He did not even tell his wife.

However, his life was so radically changed that his wife began to ask him what had happened to him. She begged and begged. Finally, after she begged for months, he told her about Christ and that he had given his life to Jesus. She, too, accepted Christ into her life.

How did this happen? It happened because God Himself gave the man a vision to seek Him. We have heard many other accounts of Muslims having dreams about Christ; these dreams touched them in such a way that the Muslims began to search for Christ.

A person of peace is a person without Christ and who has an empty hole in his or her heart. The Holy Spirit is preparing these people to hear the gospel. Our responsibility is to find those hearts He has prepared.[lxxxvi]

Chapter 13

Show God's Love
in a Practical Way

While my wife, Barbara, and I were walking along the road in India, a young woman with a basket on her head walked in front of us. The basket was piled high with wet cow manure. The manure would be mixed with dry hay and formed into large patties for people to use for fuel for cooking.

For any woman in India to drop anything off of her head is very un-usual, but on this day it happened right in front of us. The basket of cow manure was upside-down on the ground. The girl began to stomp and cry out. She was frustrated that after spending her morning in the hot sun gathering this wet cow dung, she once again would have to pick it up.

In our worldwide church-planting training conferences Barbara does a presentation on doing acts of kindness to show God's love in a practi-cal way.

After I saw the girl drop her basket, I said to Barbara, "Well, Barbara, are you going to practice what you preach?"

That day Barbara had not been thinking of putting her hands in wet cow manure! But both of us walked up beside the young woman, put our hands down into the wet cow manure, and placed it all back on her basket.

We then followed the girl to her village. She began to tell the villagers what had happened. As we entered into the village, a young man ran over to the well to pump water for us to wash our hands. A woman brought out some soap; another woman brought out a towel. In a few moments a man brought out tea to share with us. They spoke Hindi. We were not able to communicate, but everyone was having a great time laughing.

Later, we returned to the village with an interpreter. The villagers all emerged and told the interpreter what had happened. After giving time for the interpreter to get to know them, we asked the villagers whether they would be interested in hearing a story about Creator God. They all were excited about hearing a story.

The men, women, young people, boys, and girls all emerged to hear the story. We told them the story of Jesus. We taught them that Jesus was born of the virgin, Mary, in Bethlehem and was called *Immanuel,* which meant "God with us". We explained about His life and teachings and that He lived a perfect life. But one day He died on a cross for our sins, was buried, and arose on the third day. We explained that Christ is alive right now and wants to live in their hearts.

One of the village women said, "We do not understand these things, but if someone would come and explain them to us, we could understand."

That is why believers in Christ must go to the world. The Holy Spirit is drawing them to God, but how will they understand what Jesus did for them if believers do not go and explain the truth? This includes Muslims.

Why were those villagers willing to allow two foreigners to tell them a story about a God in whom they did not believe? What draws people to God? The answer, of course, is the Holy Spirit.

What about God makes people want to know Him? The fact that He is our Creator? The fact that he provided forgiveness for our sins? The fact that He is all-powerful, all-knowing, and eternal?

For each individual on this earth the answers may differ, but the love of God is one unique characteristic about God that touches the hearts of people in a profound way and makes us want to know Him.

God is love.

Allah of the Koran is not a God of love. He is so transcendent that he cannot love people. People cannot know nor love Allah. I once asked some Islamic scholars whether Allah loves sinners. The response was, "No, he hates sinners"—not so with the God of the Bible.

Jesus says that one distinctive characteristic sets His followers apart from those who follow every other religion. In John 13:35 Jesus says, "*By this all men will know that you are my disciples . . ..*" So what is "*this*"? What sets us apart from others who follow their faith? The end of that verse says, " *. . . if you love one another.*" Love is the distinctive characteristic that sets born-again believers in Christ apart from the rest of the world.

Jesus sums up the entire law and all of the commandments into two commandments. An expert in the law asks Jesus, "*Which is the greatest commandment in the Law?*" (Mt. 22:36) *Jesus replied: "'Love the Lord your God with all your heart and with all your soul and with all your mind.' This is the first and greatest commandment. And the second is like it: 'Love your neighbor as yourself.' All the Law and the Prophets hang on these two commandments*" (Mt. 22:37-40).

Islam has only law; Muslims are expected to obey these laws. The goal of Islam is to implement Islamic law over every nation, but love is not a part of it.

Jesus defines our entire moral duty as love for God and love for one's neighbor. When we love, this defines us as followers of Christ. But this is not *"love"* as the world thinks of love. Jesus describes the kind of love about which He is speaking. In verse 34 Jesus says, *"A new commandment I give you: Love one another."* Then He tells us how we are to love, *"As I have loved you, so you must love one another."*

We are to *love one another*, love our neighbor, <u>as Christ loves us</u>. To be recognized as different we must love in the same way that Jesus loves us. So the question then becomes, "How does Jesus love us?" To be able to answer that completely, as John says, *" . . . the world itself could not contain the books that would be written"* (John 21:25).

At the time Jesus explains these things to His followers, the commandment to love is not a new one. In answering the question Jesus quotes the Old Testament. So why does He say, *"a new commandment I give you"*? John MacArthur says, "Jesus' command regarding love presented a distinctly new standard for two reasons: 1) it was sacrificial love modeled after His love, and 2) it is produced through the New Covenant by the transforming power of the Holy Spirit."[lxxxvii]

Christ's love for us not only is sacrificial but also is unconditional.

Jesus loves us unconditionally.

His love for us does not depend on us. It matters not where we were born, what color we are, what language we speak, or what job we do. Jesus loves us the same whether we follow Him or whether we choose to reject Him; He still loves us (Mt. 9:9-13).

Jesus asks Matthew to follow Him. Matthew is an outcast in his time — a "sinner". But Jesus loves Matthew. Jesus sees a man who is hurting, rejected, and lost. Jesus asks Matthew to follow Him. He extends friendship to Matthew.

Jesus sees Matthew and in him sees a man that He loves so much, He is willing to die for him. Jews shun Matthew; they will not have anything to do with Him. The love of Jesus is so different that it touches Matthew's life. After this he never is the same.

The woman at the well certainly is burdened with guilt and shame. She purposely goes to the well at a time in which no one else will be there to avoid the condemning glances and perhaps words that are certain to be said to her. Not only does Jesus express love to her by talking to her, but He shows her that her life has great value to Him. He shows concern for her soul. His acceptance of her wipes away her fear so that she shares about Jesus unashamedly to the entire city .

Jesus loves us sacrificially.

Even when Jesus wants some time alone, He always is ready and willing to help those who approach Him. When those in need approach Jesus, He always gives of Himself. He gives His time and energy. Jesus feels compassion and reaches out to touch the hurting, lame, and lost. He never is too busy to help anyone (Mt. 14:13-14).

To love does not require money, but it does require time and energy. The Bible commands us to carry each other's burdens. When someone is hurting or in need, it requires a great deal of emotional energy to walk with him or her in the midst of that person's pain and crisis.

Sometimes for someone to get better takes a long time; we have to walk with him or her for months or even years. Are we willing to give up our time to invest in the life of another? Are we willing to sacrifice our lives to show the love of God?

In Luke 10:29 an expert in the law asks Jesus, in effect, if I am to love my neighbor, then *who is my neighbor?*" Jesus answers by telling a parable that demonstrates love a Samaritan expresses for a Jew, a hated enemy.

Jesus is saying that our love is to be unconditional—to love our most hated enemy. As followers of Jesus we have no choice about whom we love. Jesus has stated clearly: we are to love all people—those of all classes and castes, friend or foe, rich or poor, clean or dirty.

The Samaritan also takes time from his schedule to care for the man and even takes him to an inn for further assistance. Jesus is saying that just as He loves us, we are to love sacrificially.[lxxxviii]

God demonstrates His love.

God's greatest expression of love is the cross. *"For God so loved the world that He gave His one and only Son, that whoever believes in Him shall not perish but have eternal life."* Today God still wants to show the world His love. How can He show His love today? He wants to do it through His disciples.

We are to love in the same way; when we do, it is so radical that the world always will take notice. Muslims are arriving in our country. When they first arrive, they are displaced; many are without their families and/or friends that they had to leave. They do not know where to shop, how to shop, or where or how to do all the document work they need to do. They have been told many negative things about Americans and the infidels. No doubt many of them are afraid of what we think about them and how we are going to treat them.

When we go out of our way to love them unconditionally and sacrificially, God's love is going to soften their hearts. Some will want to know why we are so different. *"By **this** all men will know that you are my disciples . . .."*

Mosab Hassan Yousee is the son of the man who started the terrorist organization Hamas. After he was released from prison, he was walking down a street in Jerusalem when he met a Christian from Great Britain. Mosab was invited to a Bible study being conducted by the YMCA at the King David Hotel.

The people there gave him a New Testament; that began a long search for the true and living God in Christ. As he shared in his book, *Son of Hamas*, the one overwhelming factor that led him to give his life to Christ was the love of Jesus.

He writes that he read Matthew 5:43-45, which says, "*You have heard it said, 'Love your neighbor and hate your enemy.' But I tell you: Love your enemies and pray for those who persecute you, that you may be sons of your Father in heaven.*"

"That's it! I was thunderstruck by these words. Never before had I heard anything like this, but I knew that this was the message I had been searching for all my life."[lxxxix]

Mosab's testimony sums it up. We can share with Muslims all day and night, but if they do not see a real and genuine love in our hearts, all will be to no avail.

Chapter 14

The Jesus Approach

Once while I was in Uganda, I caught a motor-bike taxi. The driver was a Muslim, so while we were riding, I began to witness to him.

He asked me, "Do you eat pork?" I responded, "No, not much."

Then I asked him, "Do you believe in slavery?" Since he was a black African, I knew what the answer would be.

He said, "No."

Then I asked the big question, "Then why do you belong to a religion whose founder, Muhammad, owned slaves, promoted slaves, and even says a slave owner can have sex with his slaves?"

He was unaware that the Koran condones slavery. *Sura* 33:50 says that Muhammad owned slaves.

A strategy I like to use to raise doubts in the mind of the Muslim about his or her own religion is to ask tough questions. Tough questions need to be asked both politely and carefully, or else the question asked will offend the person.

I call this approach "the Jesus approach", because this is exactly what

Jesus does in Scripture. To make His point, He asks questions. A good example of this is Luke 9:20, "*'But what about you?' He asked. 'Who do you say I am?'*"

The first rule of thumb is never to tell or try to teach a Muslim what he or she believes about Islam. Just ask thought-provoking questions in a very loving, gentle, and kind way. Formulate almost all of the thought-provoking questions from the Koran and simply ask the person to explain the verses.

For example, *Sura* 4:34 says, "As to those women on whose part ye fear disloyalty and ill-conduct, admonish them (first), (next), refuse to share their beds, (and Last) spank them (lightly)". In sharing this Scripture with a person you might say, "Let me please ask you, do you believe that a man should beat his wife?"

This is a very good question to ask a Muslim woman. If she says, "no", then gently ask her whether she believes that God really said this. If she says, "no", then ask her whether she believes the Koran really is from God.

We now will examine good, tough questions to be asked in a loving way. I have arranged them according to various topics. The Holy Spirit can use your posing these questions to create some doubt as to the validity of Islam's prophet, Muhammad, the Muslim scriptures, and Islam itself. Be selective and be sensitive.

A person should not feel obligated to ask all of these questions to every Muslim he or she meets. Allowing the Holy Spirit to lead is very important. I have listed important questions, which are arranged by topics. Feel free to use them and to create others.

Questions about Muhammad

To a Muslim avoid saying anything negative about Muhammad. If a person does this, he or she will lose the Muslim as a friend and will lose a chance to share the gospel. However, raising doubts about whether Muhammad was a true prophet is necessary. This can be done by asking good questions in a very polite manner.

Sura 40:55 "Patiently, then, persevere: for the Promise of Allah is true: and ask forgiveness for thy fault, and celebrate the praises of thy Lord . . .."

Sura 48:2 "That Allah may forgive thee thy faults of the past and those to follow;"

Muhammad had to ask forgiveness of his sins. Jesus was perfect and did not sin. *Sura* 3:46 says, "He shall speak to the people in cradle and in maturity, and he shall be (of the company), of the righteous." If this is true, how could Muhammad be a greater prophet than Jesus?

Sura 4:3 Men can not have more then four wives. Muhammad had at least twelve. How can he be an example for us since he did not obey the law of marriage in the Koran?

Muhammad led raiding parties to steal from caravans arriving from Syria. He said that Allah gave him permission to rob these caravans on their route to Mecca. *Sura* 9:74 says, "O prophet, contend against the infidels and be rigorous with them." If he is to be a model for human-kind, does robbing caravans exemplify good character?

Sura 8:41 Muhammad was allowed to keep one-fifth of all the spoils for himself, but he did have to give the rest to his men. How can Muhammad be a moral example for humanity since he was involved in raiding and stealing from these caravans?

Sura 33:50 Muhammad owned slaves. Do you believe in slavery? If not, then why would you follow a person who claimed to be a prophet and who did own slaves?

Sura 3:181-184 Muhammad did not do any miracles. The *Hadiths*

(Muslims traditions) say he did. These traditions were composed 100 to 200 years after Muhammad. How do you explain this contradiction? Do you think they were made up?

Sura 2.136 The Lord does not make any distinction between the prophets. Islam promotes Muhammad to be the greatest prophet. Does not promoting Muhammad to this higher status contradict the Koran itself on this matter? Truly, should no distinction be made between any of the prophets as this verse teaches?

When Muhammad was 50-years old, his wife, Khadija, died. After her death he married another woman who was only 6-years old. Her name was Aisha. He consummated the marriage with Aisha when she was 9 years of age. Muhammad's behavior is supposed to be a model for all Muslims. Do you believe you would want a 50-year old man marrying your 9-year-old daughter?

Questions about the Koran

The Koran is the Holy Book for Muslims. Many will kill others if they desecrate it in any way. Treat the Koran with respect even though you believe it to be a false book from a false prophet.

Your purpose in asking the following questions is to educate average Muslims about their Holy Book which they more than likely have never read. They likely have no idea what the Koran actually says about numerous issues and topics.

The second purpose is to create a seed of doubt in the Muslim mind about the origin of the Koran. Is it a book from God or given to Muhammad by a demon? As Christians we believe it was from a demonic source, but you only can allow the Holy Spirit to use you to convince Muslims of this. You do this by asking tough questions in a respectful and polite manner.

Muhammad claimed to receive special revelations, which now are the

Koran. How do you know that God was the one speaking to him?

In the Koran some verses abrogate (cancel out) other verses. A later revelation cancels out a former one. Since the Koran is supposed to be eternal, authored by Allah, how can these revelations change and even be eliminated?

More than 100 war verses are in the Koran. For example, *Sura* 2:191 says to kill infidels everywhere you find them. "And slay them wherever ye catch them, and turn them out from where they have turned you out; fight them not at the Sacred Mosque unless they first fight you there; but if they fight you slay them such is the reward of those who suppress faith". How can Islam be considered a religion of peace when so many verses command Muslims to kill infidels?

Sura 47:4-6 instructs cutting the heads off infidels. Do you believe that you should take up the sword, fight, and cut the heads off of people who are not Muslims? Can you explain this verse?

Sura 9:29 says Jews must pay a tax for not being a Muslim. Do you believe this is fair and just?

Sura 2:63-65 teaches that disobedient Jews will be transformed into pigs. Do you believe this?

Sura 5:13 says Allah has cursed Jews. Do you believe this?

Sura 23:14 People originated from and were formed from a blood clot. Do you know any scientist that believes that?

Some Muslim scholars claim that beauty and eloquence prove that the Koran is from God. In English the writings of Shakespeare also are writings of beauty and eloquence. Would not Shakespeare's writing be equally of God as well if this is the reason to claim that God is the Koran's original source?

Questions about the Bible

Sura 5:46 says, "The Law that had come before him: We sent him the Gospel: therein was guidance and light, and confirmation of the Law that had came before him: a guidance and an admonition to those who fear Allah." Do you believe the Bible gives guidance and light?

The Koran also tells people who have doubts about their faith to go to the Bible for the answers. *Sura* 10:94 says, "If thy wert in doubt as to what We have revealed unto thee, then ask those who have been reading the Book from before thee: The Truth has indeed come to thee from thy Lord: so be in nowise of those in doubt." Do you believe that you should go to the Bible about your doubts and faith in God?

The Bible originally was written in Hebrew and Greek before Muhammad was born. The versions we have today are exactly like the copies that were around when Muhammad lived. So, how can you say they were changed? Who changed them? When were they changed?

Questions about Women

Sura 4:15-16 and 24:2 By being under house arrest women should be punished for committing adultery. Do you agree with this? Should men also be punished equally for adultery?

Sura 2:282 A woman's witness and word is half of that a man. Do you believe this?

Sura 4:11 A woman gets half the inheritance of a man. Do you believe this?

Sura 4:34 Women are to be beaten if they disobey their husbands. Do you believe this?

Sura 4:43 Touching a woman can make a man ceremonially unclean until he washes before prayer. Do you believe this?

Sura 5:6 Touching a woman can make a man unclean. Do you believe this?

Questions about Slavery

Sura 33:50 Muhammad owned slaves. Do you believe in slavery? Since Muhammad owned slaves, should we own them as well?

Sura 24:33 Slaves should not be forced into prostitution unless they are willing to do so. Do you believe this?

Questions about Sharia Law

Do you believe in Sharia law?

Do you believe that Sharia law does not heed to separation of church and state? Should all peoples in all countries heed to Islamic law in violation of their own faith, government, or independent traditions?

Under Sharia law (*Sura* 4:14-15) if she commits adultery a woman is to spend the rest of her life under house arrest. Do you believe this?

Sura 4:34 says that women are to be beaten if they do not obey their husbands. Do you believe this?

Suras 2:216, 4:95, 8:39, 9:73, and 47:4-6 command all Muslims to fight against unbelievers and even to cut off the heads of infidels. Do you believe this?

Bukhari 8, 82, 17 (The Hadiths) says to cut off the hands and feet, gouge out the eyes, and then kill anyone who leaves Islam. Do you believe this?

Sura 4:34 says that men are superior to women. Do you believe this?

Questions about *Jihad*

Jihad is defined as a "Holy War". Do you believe that a true God would declare war on people?

Sura 9:5 is known as the *Verse of the Sword*. It says, " . . . fight and slay the pagans wherever you find them. And seize them, beleaguer them, and lie in wait for them in every stratagem (of war); but if they repent and establish regular prayers and practice regular charity, then open the way for them: for Allah is oft-forgiving, Most Merciful." Do you believe Muslims should practice this verse?

Questions about Jesus

How can Muhammad be greater than Jesus when Muhammad asked for forgiveness of sins but Jesus never did? (*Sura* 48:2)

Sura 3:45 says that *Isa* is called *Messiah*. What does that mean?

Sura 3:45 says that Jesus was born of a virgin named Mary. If Jesus indeed was born of a virgin, who was His father? Why is Jesus the only one of the prophets who was born of a virgin? Do you know of any other prophet that did not have an earthly father?

Sura 4:157 says that Jesus did not die. If Jesus didn't die, then what happened to Him?

The disciples of Jesus were eyewitnesses of the crucifixion of Jesus. How then could they have not known who was on the cross?

No first-century testimonies gave doubts as to the death of Jesus on the cross. How can someone explain this?

Josephus, a historian in the time of Jesus, the Jewish Talmud, and Syriac Manuscripts all recognize that Jesus was crucified. Since these sources were not friendly toward the new Christian faith, how do you explain their testimony in light of the Koran's claim that Jesus did not die?

Since crucifixion was a very common practice, how could the Roman soldiers have been mistaken about the identity of the one they were crucifying?

How could Pilate have been fooled about the identity of Jesus when he took great care in making sure Jesus indeed was the one who was to be killed? \The Koran says that Allah will exalt those who follow *Isa*. Doesn't that mean that Christians, because they follow Jesus, are the ones God will exalt?

Salvation

The Bible teaches that all are sinners (Rom. 3:23). Do you agree?

The Bible teaches the only payment for sin is death (Rom. 6:23). Do you agree with this?

The Bible teaches that God loves you. Do you believe that God knows you by name and loves you?

The Bible teaches that God wants to give you eternal life as a free gift (Eph. 2:8-9). Do you believe this?

The Bible teaches that Jesus Christ died on a cross to make the payment for your sins because He loves you (Rom. 5:8). Do you believe this?

The Bible teaches that after He died, Christ rose from the dead and that He is alive right now and wants to live in your heart. Do you agree with this?

The Bible teaches that you can trust Christ as your Lord and Savior and by faith invite Him, by His Spirit, to enter into your life (John 1:12).

The Bible teaches that if you will confess Jesus as your Lord and believe in your heart that God has raised Him from the dead, you will be saved (Rom. 10:9). Would you be willing to pray and give Jesus Christ your life and trust Him as your Savior?

If the person says "yes", you may want to share the six verses used in the appendix of this book, "How to Have Eternal Life".

My dear Muslim evangelist friend, Dennis Rasche, when he is working with Muslims uses an approach he calls "The Trail of Blood". To demonstrate that the shedding of blood is necessary for the remission of sin he uses the following story from the Koran and the Bible:

1. Adam and Eve: *Sura* 2:34-39; 7:11-30; and Genesis 3.
   Note: Eve tried to cover up her sin and shame by shedding the blood of an animal.
2. Abraham: *Sura* 2:126; 43:57-66; 37:106-108; 16:1201-121; and Genesis 22. Share the story of Abraham's willingness to sacrifice his son.
3. Moses: *Sura* 2:40-62; 7:103-146. The Koran leaves out the Passover, so use your Bible to explain this part of the story.

After you share these verses, you then can read to the person the story of the crucifixion and resurrection of Christ. When you do this, use John 18-20. Explain how He was the Lamb of God Who shed His innocent blood for our sins.

Chapter 15

Sharing the Gospel

Different ways to share the gospel with Muslims exist. No one way or formula is correct. In this book I will suggest a few. Every person is different. Every case is different; I have found no set formula in sharing the gospel with Muslims.

Share Your Testimony

While we were in West Africa, Barbara and I were sharing Christ with a former Muslim who had become a follower of Christ. We will call him Lazarus. He grew up in a Muslim family and had become deathly ill. His Christian friends prayed over him; by the power of Jesus Christ he was healed. As a result he gave his life to Jesus. While with Lazarus I met a vendor on a street and asked whether we could talk. At that moment the vendor did not have any customers. He was very happy to talk to us about God.

Since Lazarus had been a former Muslim, I asked him whether he would share his testimony about how he had become a believer in Christ. His testimony was very powerful; God used it to enable us to introduce the Bible studies with the Muslim vendor.

The purpose of a testimony is to share a personal experience. It is one's witness to the reality and power of Jesus Christ. A person might argue about things that have happened to other people, but arguing with someone about one's own experience is difficult. In Acts 22:1-16 and Acts 26:9-23 the apostle Paul tells about his story of how he accepted Christ and what happened after he found Him.

Paul's testimony can be divided into four parts; this makes it a model after which to share one's testimony.

> **Paul's Model**
> A. How was my life before I knew Jesus? Tell about your attitudes, lifestyles, and sins (Acts 22:1-5 and 26:4-11).
> B. How did I realize my need for Jesus? (Acts 22:6-8 and 26:12-15).
> C. Where and how did I accept Christ? (Acts 22:6-10 and 26:13-18).
> D. How has my life been different since I accepted Christ? (Acts 22:10-21 and 26:19-23)[xc.]

Always conclude by saying, "I now have assurance of eternal life. May I explain to you what the Bible says about how you may have the assurance of eternal life as well?"

This kind of sharing builds a bridge between you and the lost person. You now are asking for permission to cross the bridge and enter into his or her personal life. The person may respond "yes" or may respond "no". If the person agrees, present the gospel to him or her. If the person says "no", then you may ask whether you can write the person's name in your Bible as a reminder to pray for him or her daily.

Prayer, Visions, Miracles, and Dreams

Once while I was inside a mosque and was sharing Christ, I simply said to the leader there, "Do you pray five times a day?"

"Yes," he responded.

I then challenged him, "When you pray, will you just simply ask God to reveal to you the truth about Jesus Christ?" (I like to ask all Muslims with whom I share to do this.)

After you, with love, share the gospel of Christ, a point will arrive in which you must leave the results to the Holy Spirit of God. God Himself prepares the hearts of Muslims by using prayer, visions, and dreams without the help of human beings.

Miracle Story

Pastor Mavriqi from the Republic of Kosovo told me the miracle story of his conversion.

> I was born on April 10, 1960, in the village of Dyz outside of Pristina, which formerly was a part of Yugoslavia. I grew up in the Muslim faith; Allah was all I knew. In 1998 the people of Serbia began to "cleanse" their country of the Kosovar people. I was targeted and tortured. After surviving terrible atrocities I was left for dead. To escape, my family, like many other families, fled to refugee camps in neighboring Albania.
>
> After being shot with a machine gun, having all my fingernails pulled out, all my fingers broken, and a cross carved into my chest, I was found by two American soldiers and taken to a hospital in Albania. In my heart I believed that a God, a God of love, was out there; I began to seek Him. One day in 1999 in desperation I cried out, "God, I want to know who You are. I want to know Your name!" After I prayed for one month, I heard a voice say, "I am Jesus Christ from Nazareth, born in Bethlehem. I want to save you." Once I knew who the "One True God" was, I welcomed Jesus into my heart. God radically changed me.

Three months after Pastor Mavriqi became a Christian, the United States liberated Kosovo and the war ended. After the Serbs were driven out of Kosova, Pastor Mavriqi returned to his hometown of Pristina. He and his family began to rebuild his home; he began a church. In the 11 years since the war ended, Pastor Mavriqi has planted five additional churches in outlying villages. He has baptized more than 2,000 people including his wife and all five of his children.

Miracles

One ministry in which I personally believe is simply to pray for the sick. You ask a Muslim with whom you are talking whether you can pray for him or her. If the person says "yes", then ask whether that individual has any needs. Often the person will mention a need to pray for a sickness. I then advise you to lay your hands on the individual (not a woman if you are a man) and pray for the person in Jesus' name. My personal belief is that God is Sovereign and He heals whom He desires, but I am responsible for praying for the person. Sometimes He heals; sometimes He does not. Why? I have no idea!

Share the Biblical View of Sin

In Islam sin often is viewed as a mistake. Teaching the biblical view of sin, which is disobedience of God, is important. Here is an in-depth Bible study about sin.

Teach the following seven points from the Bible:

1. We are sinners by nature. This is because of an original sin. *Original sin* refers to the original sinful state and condition in which we are born. Sin originates from Adam, the original root of the human race. Sin is present in the life of every individual from the time of a person's birth. Sin is the inward root of all the actual sins that defile the life of a human being. It refers to the corruption of the entire nature of people (Eph. 2:1-3).

2. We are sinners by choice. Muslims believe we sin because of our weakness or forgetfulness. In Psalm 51 the Bible uses these three words for sin.

Transgression: *pasha* in verse 1. The word *to transgress* means "to cross over a line". In other words, the person knows what he/she is about to do is wrong and crosses over the line anyway (Rom. 2:23; 5:14; Gal. 3:19).

Iniquity: *awon* in verse 2 means "crookedness". The idea is like dropping a plumb line; one can see how crooked a wall really is. A polished mason will drop a plumb line against a wall to see whether the wall really is straight. The plumb line will tell the mason whether the wall is crooked. God is saying that when He drops His plumb line, it will show that every person is crooked.

Sin: hatah in verse 2 carries the idea of "missing the mark". The Greek word in the New Testament is *harmartia*, which also means to "miss the mark" (Rom. 3:23 and 14:23). Once while we were in the nation of Bhutan, we were traveling up the mountain and saw some men shooting their bows and arrows. We stopped our car; I asked whether I could try and hit their target 200 yards away. My arrow went about 40 yards. I missed the mark badly. That is a picture of how we have missed God's mark and how all have sinned.

3. Teach what Jesus taught about sin:

> Matthew 12:34 People are basically evil.
> Mark 7:20-23 People are capable of evil deeds.
> Mark 1:15 People need repentance from sin.
> Luke 19:10 People are lost.
> Luke 15:10 People are sinners.

Jesus often used metaphors that illustrate what sin can do in one's life:

Matthew 9:12 Sickness
Matthew 23:16-26 Blindness
Luke 7:23-48 All are guilty of sin before God.
John 8:34 We are in bondage to sin.
John 8:12; 12:35-46 We are living in darkness.

Compare these statements of Jesus to the Muslims' belief that Adam made a mistake. Yet, it could not have been a "mistake" even by their own measurements, because the *Sura* 7:20 says that even Satan warned Adam beforehand. Thus, he committed a "transgression".

4. Sin is a principle in humanity. Sin not only is an act but also is a principle that dwells in humanity. In Romans 7:14, 17-25 the Apostle Paul refers to this struggle with the sin principle. Galatians 3:22 says that all people have this sin nature. It is described as a power that deceives people and leads them to destruction (Heb. 3:13) Jesus also refers to *sin* as a "condition" or "characteristic" quality (John 9:41, 15:24, 19:11).

5. Sin is rebellion against God. Another Greek word for *sin* is *anomia*, which means "lawlessness" (1 John 3:4). It is a sign of the last days (Mt. 24:12).

6. Sin consists of wrongful acts toward both God and others.
Romans 1:18 (NKVJ) refers to *ungodliness and unrighteousness of men*. *Ungodliness* refers to our failure to obey God and to keep His commandments related to Him (Ex. 20:1-11). *Unrighteousness* is seen in our failure to live righteously toward others (Ex. 20:12-17).

7. The only payment God will accept for sin is death by blood.
Death is "separation"; in the Bible we see three kinds of death:
Physical: Our spirits separate from our bodies and live forever either in
          heaven or hell.
Spiritual: Emptiness in the soul while one lives on earth.
Eternal: Eternal hell or separation from God.

Thus someone must die for sin. Romans 6:23 (NASB) says, *For the wages of sin is death . . ..* A "payday someday" will occur. Muslims do believe in a judgment day. They believe that if they have been good, they "may" get to enter into Paradise. However, the Bible teaches that the payment for sin is not good works but death.

Therefore, Jesus died on a cross to pay the payment for sin for us in our place. Why? John 3:16 says, *"For God so loved the world . . . ".* God loves you. This also is a foreign concept to Islam. Muslims are taught that they can not know God personally. Yet the Bible teaches that each of us can have a personal relationship with God; He does love all of us, no matter what.

Continue to share, *"God so loved the world that He gave his one and only son, that whoever believes in Him shall not perish but have eternal life."*

Teach that Jesus died the death by blood that God requires as a payment for sin. Romans 6:23 says, *For the wages of sin is death, but the gift of God is eternal life through Christ Jesus our Lord.*

Share with the person Romans 5:8, *God demonstrates his own love for us in this: While we were still sinners, Christ died for us.*

Second Corinthians 5:21 says, *God made him who had no sin to be sin for us, so that in him we might become the righteousness of God.*

Isaiah 53:6 says, *We all, like sheep, have gone astray, each of us has turned to his own way; and the Lord has laid on him the iniquity of us all.*

After you have shared these seven truths, leave the results to God.

Share the Biblical View of Atonement for Sins

Muslims do not believe that Jesus died for our sins. Explaining in detail why Jesus died on the cross may be necessary. The following explanation can be used to help Muslims understand the purpose of the death of Christ on the cross. The stories and illustrations are meant to highlight these spiritual truths. Feel free to use these illustrations or your own personal stories.

Almost two thousand people had gathered in the city plaza of Neponecema, Minas Gerais, Brazil, to see the *Jesus* film produced by Campus Crusade for Christ. That evening I would show the final part of the movie, which depicts the crucifixion of Christ, bring a brief message about the cross, and invite people to give their lives to Jesus as their Lord and Savior.

Everyone's attention was captured by the film. No one was moving. Every eye followed the scene that showed the Roman soldiers driving nails into the hands and feet of Jesus. As the nails pierced Jesus' feet, many people in the crowd began to weep. The eyes of others were squeezed tightly shut, as though they could vicariously feel the pain that Jesus had endured. Throughout the crowd emotions were high.

Suddenly a man ran toward our truck. On top of the truck we had built a metal frame for the customized screen that had been created for the purpose of showing this film in open-air settings. Before anyone could move to stop him, this man leaped up onto the truck and with both his hands grasped the screen. As he shook the screen back and forth, he shouted in Portuguese, *"Mate me! Mate me! Mate me!"*

These are the Portuguese words for, "Kill me! Kill me! Kill me!"

He did not want Jesus to die. He wanted to die in His place.

The man got it wrong. He wanted to die in Jesus' place, but 2,000 years ago, our Lord had already died in his place and in ours. By going to the cross Jesus was saying, "Kill me! Kill me! Kill me!"

Sin requires the payment of a penalty. This payment is death. For our sins to be forgiven, someone has to die. We cannot pay the penalty for sin and have any hope.

God's good news is this: Christ died in our place. He paid the price for us.

His was no ordinary death. The gospel—the good news—is summed up in 1 Corinthians 15:3-4, . . . *that Christ died for our sins according to the Scriptures, and that He was buried, and that He was raised on the third day according to the Scriptures.*

Men shouted, "Kill Jesus!"

The angry mob, the religious leaders, or the Roman soldiers were not the ones who were in control of what happened at the cross. God the Father was allowing His Son, Jesus, to die and to pay the penalty for the sins of all humankind. The purpose of Jesus' being sent to earth was to die for our redemption; it was the only way.

Jesus died voluntarily. He did for us what we could not do for ourselves. He died in our place.

He not only died for us, but He also conquered death and is wonderfully alive. This is why He alone can say, "*I am the way, and the truth, and the life; no one comes to the Father but through Me*" (John 14:6).

What happened on the cross must be understood and applied in our lives, because it is the key element of the Christian life. Apart from this, one cannot possibly become a Christian and live a victorious life. At the cross we were redeemed; our salvation was secured.

God bought every one of us with the blood of Jesus Christ. Now, as a believer, each of us belongs to Him. You and I are His adopted children and citizens of His Kingdom.

Three Biblical terms—*reconciliation, redemption,* and *justification*—clearly explain what the death of Christ on the cross accomplished for you and me and why Jesus is the only Way.

Reconciliation

Pig Eye

During the Vietnam War, when a North American pilot was shot down and captured by the Viet Cong, he was treated as an enemy. No pardon and no forgiveness occurred. Normally, the prisoner was tortured.

Captain Howard Rutledge shared his experiences of being tormented in the prison that was called the Hanoi Hilton. He recalled one particular North Vietnamese soldier whom the prisoners named Pig Eye.

Pig Eye would force Captain Rutledge to sit on the ground in a torturous position. His legs would become so swollen that he was not able to extend them. The cruel interrogator then would place one of his heavy boots on his prisoner's knee and force it downward. Afterward he would chain the suffering American's legs together in stocks. A cane and heavy rope were used to lock the ankles in place. Next, he would tie his victim's wrists behind his back. A guard would put his foot into the secured man's back and pull on the rope until the bound arms were almost separated from their sockets.

Captain Rutledge said he could feel the rope cutting his wrist to the bones. The pain was so great that he would ask God to let him slip into unconsciousness.[xci]

This is how people treat their enemies. We can be thankful that God is different. When His enemies turn to Him, they are reconciled by what Christ did on the cross. This is His good news for all people.

In Romans 5:10 (NASB) Paul was inspired to write, *For if while we were enemies we were reconciled to God through the death of His Son, much more, having been reconciled, we shall be saved by His life.*

Commenting on this, William Barclay wrote, "The essence of Christianity is the restoration of a lost relationship."[xcii]

When the New Testament speaks of *reconciliation*, it is referencing a broken relationship between two people who know each other personally. A barrier has been erected between two individuals to the point that one looks on the other as an enemy. To eliminate that barrier is to restore the relationship completely. This is what being reconciled means.

Reconcile carries the idea of change.[xciii] On the cross of Christ, God was changing our relationship with Him from hostility to peace.

A.T. Robertson, a noted Greek scholar, says, "Paul did not conceive that it was his or our work to reconcile God to us. God already took care of this himself."[xciv]

The hostility which we have toward God can be removed only by one way. God Himself took the initiative. He sent Christ to die on the cross for our sins. Through His death the barrier between God and humanity was torn down.

In 2 Corinthians 5:19 (NASB) Paul wrote, *That God was in Christ reconciling the world to Himself, not counting their trespasses against them, and He has committed to us the word of reconciliation.*

Christianity's primary message is this: Jesus of Nazareth died on a cross to destroy the barrier between God and people. Through His sacrificial death the barrier of sin was removed. Now people can approach God, be forgiven, and have our relationship with God restored.

In 2 Corinthians 5:17 (NASB) the Bible says, *Therefore if anyone is in*

Christ, he is a new creature; the old things passed away; behold, new things have come.

As believers, each of us can only have the cleansing of sin and a sense of reconciliation with God on the basis of the finished work of Christ on the cross.

Redemption

<u>The Trail of Tears</u>
In the 15th century lived a people group called the *Xwedah*. Today they are known as the *Quidah*, a French word which means "help". They can be found in the West African nation of Benin.

A Xwedah king, Kpasse, built a palace near the beach so he could better monitor his field workers. This is the site of the present city of Quidah. When Europeans first arrived in West Africa, King Kpasse's farm became their main trade center. The place was marked for infamy.

A Spanish priest, Bartholome Las Cassas, observed the strength of the African people. He was desperate to save the natives of the Americas from forced labor by their European conquerors. He successfully proposed to replace them with African workers. Pope Nicolas V signed the first slave trade agreement in 1454. This launched centuries of living hell for Africans.

From that point, millions of Africans were killed or deported to work as slaves in the newly conquered Americas. They were used to fuel the agricultural economies of Brazil, the United States, and the Caribbean. Local kings soon saw how they could benefit from this horrible business of selling men and women. To expand their kingdoms they needed the guns, cannons, and gunpowder that the Europeans brought them. To secure these they sold the captives to the white traders.

In 1727 King Agadja conquered Quidah. He made it the center of his trade in human cargo with the Europeans. At first he was content to sell defeated enemies, but his consumers were greedy. They demanded more and more slaves. Soon, commando units were raiding villages, and capturing men, women, boys, and girls. Anyone who resisted was killed.

In chains, these captives were marched to Quidah in what now is South Benin. They were made to walk only at night. This not only was done to escape the tropical heat but also to keep captives from finding their way back to their villages. Crying in pain and despair, these prisoners were hidden in the bush during the daylight. From the moment of their capture, these prisoners received no salvation and no mercy. Many of these people died before they ever reached Quidah.

Once there, slave traders from Portugal, France, England, Holland, and Denmark would bid for these people while everyone stood under a huge tree in the center of the city. From this market the slaves were led down a path to the ocean, where the ships were waiting to haul them to foreign lands. They were allowed one last stop at what was called "The Tree of Return." They were allowed to walk around the tree three times in the hope that their spirits one day would return to Africa. This was their last ritual before they passed through the "Door of No Return."[xcv]

Suppose a slave was taken to the Americas and bought by a good and merciful man. The master would then tell the slave, "I have purchased you with my money, but I am going to give to you a gift of freedom."

A lost sinner is in exactly the position of the slaves that I have just described. Without Christ people are without hope. When they turned their backs on God and became the slaves of sin, they passed through the "Door of No Return." But, miracle of miracles, Jesus paid the highest price possible—the price of His own blood—to purchase the slave! Because of this we have hope where no hope existed. The sinner can be set free.

This is redemption—for a price, buying a hopeless slave and setting that slave free.

Redeem is another word that describes what happened when Jesus died on the cross. As it is used in the Bible, this word means "to free by ransom."

An Old Testament law says that if a man owns a bull that has a habit of goring people, the animal must be securely confined. If the owner does not keep his bull penned up and it kills someone, both the bull and the owner are to be stoned to death. However, this law allows for a payment to be made to redeem the man's life. He is required to pay whatever is demanded of him by the offended party (Ex. 21:29-30).

Job declared, "*I know that my Redeemer lives*" (Job 19:25 NASB).

In the New Testament the word *redeem* is used with the reference to slave markets. The thought was that a payment had to be made in order for a slave to be freed.

Jesus said, "*For even the Son of Man did not come to be served, but to serve, and to give His life a ransom for many*" (Mark 10:45 NASB).

Paul used this word when he wrote, *In Him we have redemption through His blood, the forgiveness of our trespasses, according to the riches of His grace* (Eph. 1:7 NASB).

Paul was saying that we are set free from slavery to sin by the sacrificial death of Christ on the cross. With His own blood Jesus paid our ransom.

In 1 Peter 1:18-19 (NASB) the Bible says, *Knowing that you were not redeemed with perishable things like silver or gold from your futile way of life inherited from your forefathers, but with precious blood, as of a lamb unblemished and spotless, the blood of Christ.*

When someone surrenders his or her life to Christ, from time to time the person still will sin, but when Jesus died on the cross, He paid for all of the person's sins, once and for eternity. Because of this the person can be cleansed and made holy before God.

Justification

A Murderer's Prayer

Our town marshal asked me to accompany him as he answered an emergency call. We drove into the darkness of the Louisiana countryside and stopped where four bodies blocked the lonely gravel road. Each of these people had been shot in the head. For many days their blood would mark the spots on which they had died.

Quickly a posse was formed to assist the police. Heavily armed and using dogs to follow the murderer's scent, these men of the posse searched throughout the night. Early the next morning they found the suspect hiding in a barn. He was taken to the Clinton Parish jail to wait for his arraignment and trial.

Since my sophomore year in high school my habit had been to preach every Sunday at the parish jail. The Sunday after the murders was no exception.

That morning I told the prisoners that whatever crimes they had committed did not matter; God would forgive them if they would repent and trust Christ as their Lord and Savior. I invited those who wanted to give their lives to Christ to kneel on the floor in front of me. Slowly, from the back of the room, a man walked forward. In front of me he dropped to his knees and began to weep. Through his tears he said, "I am sorry for what I did. Will God forgive me?"

Amazed, I realized that the broken man before me was the murderer of the people whose bodies I had seen on that country road.

"Yes," I assured him. "No sin exists that God cannot forgive."

That day I watched as a murderer prayed and asked Christ to forgive him and enter into his heart.

Was this conversion real? Only he and God know that. I do know this: if the man meant what he prayed, God took his sin of murder and placed it on Christ. On the cross Christ bore the man's sin of murder.

When Jesus died on the cross, He was punished for the murders that man committed. He was judged and condemned for killing those people. All of the prisoner's guilt was placed on Jesus, even though Jesus was righteous and without sin.

Here is what happened. In His body Christ suffered all the guilt and punishment which the murderer deserved.

Remember the introduction to this chapter and the lesson of Romans 5:1. When the guilty man cried out and received Jesus as his Lord and Savior, God placed in him His own righteousness.

When that murderer goes before God the Father on judgment day, He will not see the man's sin of killing, nor will He see any other sin. In the person He will see the righteousness of Christ. The Father will look into his heart and see His Son, Jesus Christ. For that reason only, He will say to him, "Welcome into My house."

The Bible calls this transfer *justification*. *Justified* is the Bible's legal term for what *being saved* means.

In *The Amplified Bible* Romans 5:1 reads, *Therefore, since we are justified (acquitted, declared righteous, and given a right standing with God) through faith, let us [grasp the fact that we] have [the peace of reconciliation to hold and to enjoy] peace with God through our Lord Jesus Christ (the Messiah, the Anointed One).*

Justification means that God will treat me "just as if I'd" never sinned and just as if I had perfectly obeyed.

When a person is justified, the guilt and penalty of that person's sin is removed and Christ's own righteousness is imparted to him or her. In other words, when God the Father looks into the heart of a repentant sinner, instead of the ugliness of his sin He sees the righteousness of His Son, Jesus Christ.

Justified is a legal term that describes what happens when a person receives Christ as his or her personal Lord and Savior (John 1:12) When someone is justified, his or her judicial standing is changed before God.

An accused man stands in court and waits for the jury to pronounce its verdict. When the foreman stands and reads "not guilty", the man instantly is declared innocent of all charges against him. He will walk out of the courtroom a free person. He is justified.

Being justified before God means more than being declared "not guilty". It means that a person is declared to be righteous. God places the perfect righteousness of Jesus Christ into a repentant sinner's heart.

Galatians 3:6 in *The Amplified Bible* reads, *Abraham believed in and adhered to and trusted in and relied on God, and it was reckoned and placed to his account and credited as righteousness (as conformity to the divine will in purpose, thought, and action).*

This word *credited* is *imputed* in the Greek New Testament (*logizomai*). It means to count, to reckon, to calculate, to compute, and to set to one's account. Abraham believed God; his act of faith was placed on deposit for him and valued as righteousness. This does not mean Abraham deserved this reward. That would be salvation by works. He simply cast all of his dependence on God and accepted God's way of salvation.[xcvi]

In Romans 4:6 and 8 (NASB), the Bible says, *Just as David also speaks of the blessing on the man to whom God credits righteousness apart from works . . . Blessed is the man whose sin the Lord will not take into account.*

Verses 22-25 (NASB) say, *Therefore it was also credited to him as righteousness. Now not for his sake only was it written that it was credited to him, but for our sake also, to whom it will be credited, as those who believe in Him who raised Jesus our Lord from the dead, He who was delivered over because of our transgressions, and was raised because of our justification.*

The words, *it was also credited to him* were not written for Abraham alone. They were also written for all of us who believe on God the Father, who raised Jesus from the dead. Because of our trust in Christ, our accounts will be credited with His righteousness.

A person may look at himself or herself and ask, "How can that be? I know myself. By nature and by choice I am a sinner. I don't deserve to be justified."

To understand the miracle of justification a person must, by faith, accept these truths. Jesus Christ lived a sinless life. He was perfect. Yet He died a criminal's death on a cross, as if He were a sinner. Why? Because, at the moment of His death, God the Father placed on Jesus all of our sin. He took on Himself the full weight of guilt that belonged to each of us. He went to the cross without sin, so that He could redeem everyone of us from the penalty and power of sin. He died for each of us individually as well as collectively.

In Romans 5:19 (NASB) the Apostle Paul wrote about this truth, *For as through the one man's disobedience the many were made sinners, even so through the obedience of the One the many will be made righteous.*

In 1 Corinthians 1:30 (NASB) we read: *But by His doing you are in Christ Jesus, who became to us wisdom from God, and righteousness and sanctification, and redemption.*

Don't misunderstand what this means. Justification does not make *a person* righteous, but each of us is *declared* righteous because of the righteousness of Christ that is in our lives as a free gift from God.

Romans 3:24 (NASB) says that we are *Being justified as a gift by His grace through the redemption which is in Christ Jesus.*

Fully digesting what is being said here is important. Justification is a gift from God. It is granted by grace—the unmerited favor of God. By definition any gift is free. It cannot be earned. A gift of grace is one that is offered not only to someone who has not earned it; the person does not deserve it.

When someone receives Christ into his or her life, two things happen. First, the person's sins leave him or her and are placed on Jesus. Secondly, the righteousness of Christ enters the sinner's heart. An exchange takes place. Christ exchanges His righteousness for the sins of the repentant sinner. What an incredible exchange this is—our sins for his righteousness!

In 1 John 5:12-13 (NASB) the Bible says, *He who has the Son has the life; he who does not have the Son of God does not have the life. These things I have written to you who believe in the name of the Son of God, so that you may know that you have eternal life.*Each of us should ask ourselves, *Do I know that I have the Son, am I justified—saved by grace through faith in Christ?* (Eph. 2:8-9).

Even a murderer can know this.[xcvii]

Share the Biblical View of Salvation

One way to explain to a Muslim these life-changing fundamentals about Christ would be to use a topical Bible study of the gospel. If you take this approach, then make sure to include the following topics. You also may want to share with the person six verses that explain how to have eternal life. This study is found in the appendix entitled "How to Have Eternal Life".

• God is Love; He loves each of us.
• We all have sinned against a Holy God.
• The payment for sin is death by blood.
• Jesus Christ paid the price of sin in our place.
• God offers eternal life to all who will trust Christ.

• To receive eternal life one must repent and trust Christ as Lord and Savior.

Repentance and Faith

Repentance means to change one's mind. When people repent, they change their minds about who God is, about sin, and about Jesus Christ. It also means *to turn*. A person turns from a self-controlled life to Jesus Christ Who is Lord. It is a rejection of a former reliance on Muhammad and good works. It is a rejection of self-reliance, reliance on rituals, prayers, festivals, and anything else a person formally has trusted to bring him or her to God.

By using self-effort no one can possibly change his or her own life. Repentance is not one's own determination to change the way he or she is living and do better. It is an intentional turning to Christ and allowing Him to take complete control of one's life. Christ does all of the changing.

Repentance and faith cannot be separated. When a person feels the conviction of sin and is drawn by the Holy Spirit, Christ enables the person to repent, turn from sin, and to commit himself or herself, by faith, to Christ.

Faith is more than an intellectual head knowledge and belief that God exists and that Jesus died for sins. Biblical faith requires a total commitment of one's life to Christ. A person must surrender to Christ as Lord and Master.

In Romans 10:9 Paul stressed that being a Christian means that a person acknowledges that Jesus is Lord. In *The Amplified Bible* that verse reads, *Because if you acknowledge and confess with your lips that Jesus is Lord and in your heart believe (adhere to, trust in, and rely on the truth) that God raised Him from the dead, you will be saved.*

This verse talks about "heart belief". To believe in one's heart that Christ does for him or her what he or she cannot do for himself or herself, which is to forgive sins and transform lives.

When someone is convinced that Jesus is Lord and confesses this openly, this person is drawn to turn in repentance from a previous self-controlled life and to surrender completely to Jesus as Lord. The person allows Christ to take absolute control of his or her life.

Most Bible scholars recognize three aspects of faith: knowledge (*notitia*), assent (*assensus*), and trust (*fiducia*). Theologian Augustus H. Strong sees knowledge as the intellectual element of faith. Assent is the emotional element; trust is the volitional element.[xcviii]

True faith involves all three elements. First, one's mind embraces the knowledge of who Christ is, that He died on a cross as a sacrifice for sins, and that He arose from the dead. Next, the person assents (agrees) to this truth in his or her heart. A person feels in his or her innermost being that this is true. Finally, the person makes a decision, by his or her own will, to commit himself or herself to Christ. The person invites Him to take control of his or her life.

Dividing Jesus into two entities, Savior *or* Lord, is impossible. He is Savior *and* Lord. No one can receive half of Jesus. A person who wants to give his or her life to Christ must accept Christ for all that He is.

Jesus also is God, King, Judge, Advocate (Supporter), and Counselor. He is the Alpha and the Omega (the Beginning and the End). Jesus is all of this and more.

When a person trusts Christ as Savior, that person must accept and trust Him for all that He is.

When a person is committed to Jesus as Lord and Savior, that individual is saved. He or she is justified and is a child of God. His or her sins are forgiven; Christ's righteousness has been planted in that person's heart.

Everything begins with one word, *surrender*. God requires unconditional surrender.

Dr. John MacArthur says, "Surrender to Jesus' lordship is not an addendum to the biblical terms of salvation: the summons to submission is at the heart of the gospel invitation throughout Scripture."[xcix]

He concludes that surrender is not an addition to faith but it is "the essence of faith."[c]

Trust is the essential factor in surrender. Rick Warren says, "You will not surrender to God unless you trust Him."[ci]

To whatever a person is surrendered defines his or her life. All of us represent the sum total of our commitments. To have purpose and meaning a person must be committed to the right thing. In this case the right thing really is not a thing but a person, Jesus Christ.

God is looking for people whom He can use. God is looking in all of our hearts to see on whom He can depend to make differences in the world for His glory. If we are Christians who want God to use us, we have one requirement. Second Chronicles 16:9 (NASB) says, *For the eyes of the LORD move to and fro throughout the earth that He may strongly support those whose heart is completely His.*

Take notice that God is looking for that person *whose heart is completely His*. In other words He is looking for a person who is totally surrendered to Him.

God has a primary purpose for our lives. He will not force Himself on anyone. He gives each of us a choice. This is where surrender (commitment) comes in. Before anything else can happen, we must know God, turn in repentance, receive Christ by faith, and be totally committed to Him as Lord. This is the most important issue in each of our lives.

Every commitment has a benefit and a cost. What's the cost of following Christ? A person who surrenders his or her life to Christ gives up the control of his or her life and puts Jesus Christ in charge.

As a person reading this book, the time may have arrived for you to think about this issue on a personal level. Have you settled this matter of Christ's Lordship and on your relationship to Him? If not, right now, you can do what I did. I approached Jesus just as I was and gave my life completely to Christ.

Before you close this book, pray simply and humbly to Jesus. From your heart say, "Lord Jesus Christ, I open my heart to you. I surrender myself to you for the rest of my life."

The path toward Lordship ends at the cross when you lay down all of your sin at the feet of Jesus. If you prayed this prayer, He has taken away the barrier between you and the Father. Now, you can be clean and holy.

Your life now will have new meaning and you will be walking in a new direction. You will see the world through new eyes. Your value system will be radically changed.

Second Corinthians 5:17 (NASB) says, *Therefore if anyone is in Christ, he is a new creature; the old things passed away; behold, new things have come.*

You have now begun a new exciting journey as God now will mold your life to become what you were created to be. Philippians 1:6 says, (NIV) *being confident of this, that he who began a good work in you will carry it on to completion until the day of Christ Jesus.*

Share about the Feast of Id

Another way is to share Christ is to use the Muslim culture to present the gospel. One such custom is the Feast of Id.

Seventy days after Ramadan is a religious feast called "The Feast of Id". Families slay an animal, preferably a ram. They remember Abraham's call to slay an animal to be slaughtered in the place of his son.[cii]

This is an opportunity to present the gospel using the story in Genesis 22:1-13. Note that Muslims believe that Ishmael is the son who was offered, even though the Bible says the son was Isaac. Personally, I would not spend my time debating this issue. Once the Muslim trusts Christ he or she then will believe the Bible to be the Word of God. But one must remember that the Muslim has been taught all of his or her life that the Bible has been corrupted, so at this point be very careful.

As you share this story then relate the truth that Jesus Christ was the Lamb of God. Show the Muslim John 1:29 and then teach the person the Scriptures about the crucifixion of Christ.

Explain the following passages
- Hebrews 4:14-16
- Hebrews 9:11-15
- Hebrews 10:1-14
- 1 Corinthians 15:3-4
- Colossians 1:13-14
- Acts 4:12
- 1 Timothy 2:5-6

Share Christ Using the Koran as a Bridge

When the Apostle Paul was in the city of Athens, he used a principle of "bridging" to bridge the pagans with whom he was ministering to the gospel. He said in Acts 17:22-23 that as he was walking around the city, he noticed many different objects of worship and even found one altar that said *to the unknown God*. He used this cultural situation to introduce the gospel of Christ. He created a bridge from the place at which they were to where he wanted to lead them. In verse 28 he quoted one of their Stoic philosophers, "*For in him we live and move and have our being.*" Again, he was bridging them. He started at the place at which their reality was and was leading them to the reality of Christ.

One of my close friends was a missionary in North Africa. He shared a unique way that his national believers use to witness for Christ. When they meet a Muslim, they begin a conversation. Then they use *Sura* 3:45 which says that Jesus (*Isa*) is the Word of God. After the Christian evangelist shows a Muslim this verse, the Christian immediately reads John 1:1 and 1:14 and explains what the phrase *Word of God* means. This leads to deeper Bible studies that treat the topics of sin and salvation in Christ.

Share the Life of Christ

Evangelistic Storying Lessons from the Book of Matthew

The lessons in the appendix are used worldwide with nonbelievers from all different religious backgrounds including Muslims.

These were written by Christy A. Brawner. She developed a series of studies on the life of Jesus Christ from His birth to His resurrection. All over the world in our ministry we are using the studies included in the following section; they are translated into many languages. This series is being powerfully used around the globe.

These seven lessons all are based on the Book of Matthew. Each lesson has the story of some aspect of the life of Jesus. Lesson one starts with His birth; the series concludes with the crucifixion and resurrection of Christ. Each lesson concludes by teaching the spiritual truths which the reader learns from the story. The spiritual truths gradually teach the seeker how to become a follower of Christ. In this way a nonbeliever is learning two things at the same time: the life of Christ and how to become a follower of Jesus and be saved.

These stories will be included at the end of this book. Anyone may use these lessons. You also can download them from our website: *www.pioneermissions.org*

APPENDIX

1. The Good News of Jesus by Christy A. Brawner

2. How to Have Eternal Life: Six Verses that Explain the Gospel

THE GOOD NEWS
OF JESUS

By Christy Akins Brawner

Evangelistic Series
Pioneer Evangelism Series
How to Use "The Good News of Jesus"

NOTE: The following lessons are summaries that take a reader through the first book of the New Testament—the Book of Matthew. They are designed to be read and studied by a person who is not familiar with the life of Jesus Christ or the Bible. A person does not need to have any previous knowledge of Christianity nor of Christ to be able to follow and understand these studies.

Before you share the story of Jesus Christ, read these suggestions and share the spiritual truths included in each lesson.

Remember always to treat every person with respect. Ask permission to tell the story and to continue each week.

Speak in a calm, conversational voice. Do not preach at an individual. These lessons are not sermons and are intended to be used in informal settings, preferably in the context of a home.

Do not argue about the truths. The Bible is the Word of God and can stand alone. It convicts each of us of truth and righteousness.

Do not judge any person nor condemn anyone for what the person believes. These lessons are designed to study the Bible and learn the biblical view of God, ourselves, and the world.

Begin each meeting with a brief word of prayer. Ask the Lord to bring understanding to the stories.

Use the following method to tell the story: Read from the booklet one sentence at a time and then in your own words explain what you just read. These stories, although familiar to a Christian, are new and to a person not familiar with the Bible often are very unusual. Stopping at the end of each sentence and/or paragraph allows a first-time listener to process and ask questions about the story as the listener has them. If available copies exist, each person ideally can follow along with his or her own copy of the study. Sometimes participants like to read outloud, but sometimes they don't. Be sensitive to the unique needs of each individual; allow the person to do what makes him or her the most comfortable.

The leader should ask the oral questions at the end of the story. The purpose for these questions is to review and check for understanding of the story—NOT for elaboration or debate.

Read the spiritual truths. Allow the group members freedom to discuss and question each spiritual truth. Be careful NEVER to argue or debate with anyone. For the participants to agree or accept the spiritual truths is not necessary. Understanding the truths as they are revealed in God's Word is of major importance. The purpose of the study is to see what the Bible is saying.

After the spiritual truths are shared, allow a time for each person to share needs and prayer requests as he or she feels comfortable sharing. Some participants may be shy at first, but encourage these people to approach God with their needs.

Pray specifically for each need and/or each person in the group.

At the conclusion of lesson seven the leader will invite the participants to accept Jesus as their Lord. But if anyone expresses interest in giving their lives to Jesus at any time during the seven weeks, the leader can share with the participant how to make Jesus his or her Lord and can give the person the opportunity to do so.

THE GOOD NEWS OF JESUS

By
Christy A. Brawner

The Birth of Jesus—Lesson 1

Matthew 1-2

So all the generations from Abraham to David are fourteen generations, from David until the captivity in Babylon are fourteen generations, and from the captivity in Babylon until the Christ are fourteen generations (Mt. 1:17).

Mary, a Jewish woman, became pregnant without having sexual relations, for she conceived of the Holy Spirit. Her fiancé, being a just man, did not want to publicly humiliate her, so he decided to break off the engagement secretly. But the same night as he was deciding to do this, an angel of the Lord appeared to him in a dream and said, "*Joseph, son of David, do not be afraid to take Mary as your wife, for that which is conceived in her is of the Holy Spirit. And she will bring forth a Son, and you shall call His name Jesus for He will save His people from their sins.*" For Mary was to be the woman of which the prophet Isaiah spoke of in the Old Testament when he said, "*Behold, the virgin shall be with child, and bear a Son, and they shall call His name Immanuel*", translated "God with us."

Joseph awoke from His dream and obeyed the angel. He married Mary, but they did not have sexual relations until after the birth of the baby. Joseph named the baby *Jesus*, according to the instructions which he had received from the angel. Now Jesus was born in the city of Bethlehem, which is located in the Province of Judea in the country of Israel; the King of Judea at that time was named Herod.

Wise men traveled from the Orient to Judea as they followed a bright star. According to their studies this star indicated that the promised king had been born in Judea. Not knowing where exactly the Child was to be found, they first went to the palace of Herod, the king of the district of Judea, and asked where the new king of the Jews had been born.

Herod was very disturbed by their story and called a secret meeting with all his religious advisers and priests. He asked these men where, according to Jewish prophecy, was the promised King of the Jews to be born. The priests told him that according to Scripture, the Promised Child was to be born in Bethlehem. Herod went to the wise men and asked them when exactly they had first seen the star. He asked this because he wanted to figure out the precise birth date of the child and calculate His age.

Herod informed the wise men in which city the baby was to be born. He also said, *"Go and search carefully for the young Child, and when you have found Him, bring back word to me, that I may come and worship Him also."*

The wise men then left the palace and continued to follow the star to Bethlehem. The star, which they had been following, went before them and stood over the house where the young Child was. They entered the house. Immediately as they saw the Child with Mary His mother, they fell down and worshiped Him. They also gave Him valuable gifts of gold, frankincense, and myrrh.

So the wise men left this place to return to their homes in the East. But before they left, they had a dream that warned them not to return to Herod and tell him how to find the child. So they went home another way.

After they left, Joseph had another dream. In this dream God warned him that Herod was going to try to take the Child and that they were to flee to Egypt. So, that very night, Joseph woke up His family; the family fled immediately. Joseph, Mary, and Jesus lived in Egypt until the death of Herod; this also was in fulfillment of the prophecy of the prophet Hosea where he said, *"Out of Egypt I will call My Son."*

Herod, after he discovered that the wise men had deceived him, became very angry. He then declared that all male babies under the age of 2 would be murdered. This was a horrifying slaughter of all the infants in Bethlehem and the surrounding towns. But an earlier Jewish prophet named Jeremiah also had foretold this tragedy.

When Herod died, an angel appeared to Joseph and told him to return to Israel. Joseph, however, was a little anxious because Herod's son was on the throne in Judea, so he moved his family to the neighboring province of Galilee to a city called Nazareth. Jesus spent his childhood in this town. This also was in fulfillment of the prophecy which said, "*He will be called a Nazarene.*"

Oral Questions

1. Who is Mary?
2. To whom did the angel appear and tell what the Child was to be named?
3. Why did wise men travel from the Orient to Judea?
4. Why did Herod want to find Jesus?
5. How did the wise men know they should go home another way and avoid Herod?
6. How did Herod attempt to kill the promised King of the Jews?
7. How did Joseph know he must flee the country and go to Egypt?
8. How did Joseph know when returning was safe?
9. Why did Joseph take his family to the neighboring province of Galilee instead of taking the family to Judea?
10. What is the name of the city in which Jesus spent his childhood?

Spiritual Truths—Lesson 1

Matthew 1-2

God is faithful and always keeps His promises. Since the creation of the first man and woman, God had promised that He would send a Savior to earth. Over the years many times He repeated this promise to many people often with many details of how this would occur. Jesus was sent to earth EXACTLY as had been predicted through the Scriptures. Let us remember in the story at least one prophecy that was fulfilled through the birth of Jesus.

In the same way God is faithful to us. In the Bible are many important promises God has made about His plan for us. He will fulfill all these promises and prophecies. Reading the Scriptures and discovering God's promises for our lives is important.

The Bible is the Word of God; everything in it is true. Through His prophets thousands of years in advance God spoke many precise details about the birth and life of Jesus. Everything occurred EXACTLY as had been prophesied

God is in control of all things. He can make things happen that are supernatural or miraculous. Several supernatural things or miracles happen in this story. Do you think God is capable of doing things that do not follow the natural laws of science? Do you believe in miracles?

God can and does communicate to people. Some believe that God created the world but doesn't care what happens here. In this story in what way did God communicate to people? God still communicates to us today. Through this study we will learn how we can have a real relationship with God.

God knows everything that is going to happen. But sometimes in His Divine wisdom He allows horrible things to occur. Herod wanted to kill the Promised King because he felt threatened by Jesus. God knew the wicked sin in Herod's heart. He knew that Herod was going to kill hundreds of helpless children. Because of the disobedience and rebellion in Herod's heart a great horror occurred. Today sometimes many horrible things happen because of disobedience and rebellion in our lives. Do you know of a modern example in which someone has been hurt because of the wickedness of another person?

People never can prevail against God and win. Herod was unable to kill the Promised Child. The only thing that he accomplished was to create a horrendous tragedy in the lives of many families. Many times today we try to defy God's laws and His will. This always brings tragedy — if not for us, for those around us who we are hurting. Can you think of a time in your own life in which you did something wrong and brought tragedy into your life? Can you think of a time in which you were hurt because of the rebellion of another person?

The priests and religious advisers knew the Scriptures about the Promised King, but they did not go to meet Jesus. Can someone be religious, know much about the Bible, and know much about Jesus Christ, but never know Him personally in his or her heart?

Jesus is *"God with us"*, or *"Immanuel"*. The angel spoke these words to Joseph; the prophet Isaiah recorded them in the Scriptures. Many people say that Jesus was a prophet. Others say that He was an angel or a good person. But the Bible teaches us that He was *"God with us."*

In the next six weeks we will try to discover Whom JESUS CHRIST really is and discover the GOOD NEWS that He brought to earth.

The Baptism of Jesus—Lesson 2

Matthew 3-4

"Repent for the kingdom of heaven is at hand" (Mt. 3:2).

These were the words that were preached by a man who could be found in the desert of Judea. This man dressed in camel's hair and a leather belt. He lived eating wild honey and grasshoppers. His name was John the Baptist. Many people from all over the area surrounding the Jordan River would go out to the desert to hear his words. Then after they listened to him speak, many would be baptized in the Jordan River and would confess their sins. Several of the religious leaders, those called *Sadducees* and *Pharisees*, also would go out to see what was happening in the desert. When John the Baptist saw them, he called them a *brood of vipers* (sons of serpents). He further said that they did not fear God because they thought themselves so religious and of such good heritage that they did not need to repent of their sins.

While John was preaching, Jesus arrived and asked John to baptize Him. At first John did not want to, because he thought he was too un-worthy to baptize Jesus. But Jesus insisted; the two of them entered into the waters of the Jordan River. When Jesus arose out of the water, the Holy Spirit descended like a dove from heaven on Him. Also, a very loud voice from heaven spoke saying, *"This is my beloved Son, in whom I am well pleased."*

After that the Holy Spirit took Jesus into the desert so Satan could tempt Him. For 40 days and 40 nights Jesus fasted from food and water. After the 40 days He was very hungry. At this time Satan ar-rived to tempt Jesus.

The Bible tells of three temptations of Jesus in the desert. In the first temptation Satan tried to get Jesus to turn some stones into bread. He claims that this would prove that He was God. Jesus answered

Satan by using the written Word of God. Secondly, Satan took Him to the roof of a temple and asked Him to jump off the edge and thus prove that He was God. But Jesus answered him again and used the written Word of God. Lastly, Satan transported Jesus to a mountain and said, "*All these things I will give You if You will fall down and worship me.*" Jesus answered him by saying, "*You shall worship the LORD your God, and Him only you shall serve.*" With this the devil left Him; the angels arrived and served Him.

After he returned from the desert, Jesus heard that John the Baptist had been thrown into jail. Jesus then went to Galilee, the province north of Judea, and left Nazareth, the city of His childhood, and moved to Capernaum. This was in fulfillment of what was spoken by the prophet Isaiah when he said, "*The land of Zebulun and the land of Naphtali, by the way of the sea, beyond the Jordan, Galilee of the Gentiles: the people who sat in darkness have seen a great light, and upon those who sat in the region and shadow of death light has dawned.*"

The Bible tells us that from this town Jesus began His public work among the people. The message that He preached was like that of John the Baptist: "*Repent, for the kingdom of heaven is at hand.*"

Oral Questions

1. Describe the man called *John the Baptist.*
2. What was the message of John the Baptist?
3. What would John the Baptist do with those who confessed their sins?
4. Why did John the Baptist not want to baptize Jesus?
5. How was Jesus baptized?
6. What happened when Jesus arose from the water?
7. Why did Jesus go to the desert?
8. What did Jesus do for 40 days and 40 nights?
9. What was one of Satan's temptations?
10. After the temptations who arrived to serve Jesus?
11. Where did Jesus go after He learned about the fact that John the Baptist was imprisoned?
12. What was Jesus' message? Who preached this same message?

Spiritual Truths-Lesson 2

Matthew 3-4

The message of John the Baptist and of Jesus was the same: *"Repent for the kingdom of heaven is at hand."*
To *repent* means to turn from the sin in your life. It means to give the complete control of your life to Jesus Christ.
Sin is disobeying God and His law.
Is repenting a very difficult thing for a person to do? What does this word mean to you? The religious leaders thought that because of their religion, they did not need to repent of their sins. They thought that they were good enough. John called these people *sons of serpents*. Are any people in the world religious enough or even good enough that they do not need to repent of their sins?

In Romans 3:23 the Bible says that *All have sinned and have fallen short of the glory of God.*

Some suggest that people do not sin; instead we make mistakes. The Bible rejects this idea. Of course we all make mistakes, but we also intentionally sin. The Bible says that we deliberately have turned from God. We have done things that fall short of God's perfection. Does anyone in the world not have sin in his or her life? Does someone exist who has not lied or cheated or stolen or hated or held bitterness in his or her heart? These are examples of sins. Does someone exist who never has disobeyed or defied God's standard of behavior or attitude? The Bible says "No". Do you agree with the Bible that we all have sin in our lives?

Jesus was baptized, but He being God never sinned. This tells us that baptism is NOT a religious ritual that can take away the sins from a person's life. If the purpose of baptism was to cleanse a person from sins, Jesus would not have been baptized, because He, being God, never has sinned.

When Jesus raised up out from the waters, the Holy Spirit descended on him like a dove. God the Father spoke from heaven and said, *"This is my beloved Son in whom I am well pleased."* Here we see the three persons of the Trinity. Who are they?

God the Father, God the Son, and God the Holy Spirit.

Some religious traditions believe many gods are in the universe. The Bible teaches that ONE God exists. He is the Creator God, a God of love, and a God who desires to have a relationship with us. He is three in one. From a human perspective this does not seem possible, because we are not three in one, but that is why we are not God—nor can we ever become God. He is superior to us in every way but loved us enough to be sent to us as a human being and to reach out to us.

Jesus was taken out to the desert to be tempted by Satan. Satan is real. He is a spirit who along with many of his spirit followers called *demons* exist in the world and can bring destruction to our lives by leading us to disobey God. Just as Jesus was tempted, Satan also tempts us. But the Bible teaches that we, unlike Christ, also are tempted by wickedness that already lives in our hearts. We are tempted do things that displease God, or to *sin*.

The prophet Isaiah prophesied that Jesus would live in the way of the sea and that He would be a light to the people who were in darkness—to those who were living in the shadow of death.

All of us, without Christ, are in darkness, but maybe you or someone you love is living in the shadow of death. Some find themselves in this situation because of drugs, others through immoral relationships, and still others are victims of violence. This verse tells us that Jesus was sent to give light to those of us in darkness. He can give freedom to those who are living in the shadow of death.

In our prayer time today let's pray for those loved ones that are living in the shadow of death. May we all find light and freedom in Jesus Christ.

The Miracles of Jesus—Lesson 3

Matthew 4-9

Follow Me, and I will make you fishers of men (Mt. 4:19).

While He was walking along the Sea of Galilee, Jesus saw two fishermen. He called them and said, *"Follow me, and I will make you fishers of men."* They immediately left their nets and followed Him. On that day, Jesus called his first four disciples: Peter, Andrew, James, and John. All of them were fishermen.

Then Jesus went through all the province of Galilee teaching in the synagogues, preaching the gospel of the kingdom, and curing all kinds of sickness and disease among the people. Wherever He went, a large multitude followed Him.

A leper approached Jesus and proceeded to worship Him. He called to Jesus and said, *"Lord if you are willing, You can make me clean."* Jesus responded, *"I am willing, be cleansed."* Immediately the leper was cleansed.

A captain of the Roman army approached Jesus. This man asked Him to cure his servant who was paralyzed and tormented. He believed in Jesus' power to cure him. Jesus told him that many people of all nationalities would eat together in the kingdom of heaven. At that same hour the servant was cured.

Another time, on the other side of the sea, were two men possessed by demons. These men were so strong and ferocious that no one could hold them down or even walk by them. They lived among the tombs.

When they saw Jesus, the demons yelled out, *"What have we to do with You, Jesus, You Son of God? Have You come here to torment us before the time?"*

In the distance was a herd of pigs. The demons begged Jesus, *"If You cast us out, permit us to go away into the herd of swine."* Jesus said to them, *"Go."* The demons immediately were expelled from the men and entered into the pigs. The pigs in turn became possessed and crazed. They violently ran down the steep cliff and crashed into the sea below. All the pigs drowned.

The pigs' owners ran and told all the inhabitants of this particular city what Jesus had done and what had happened to the demon-possessed men. The townspeople asked Jesus to leave their region.

He left by boat and returned to His own city. Soon after this He met a man named Matthew. Matthew worked as a tax collector for the government. Jesus said to him, "*Follow Me.*" Matthew got up immediately and followed Him.

So Jesus and His followers went to eat dinner that night with the tax collectors and other townspeople who had bad reputations. When the religious leaders—the Pharisees—saw this, they asked Jesus' disciples, "*Why does your Teacher eat with tax collectors and sinners?*"

When Jesus heard this comment, He answered, "*Those who are well have no need of a physician, but those who are sick. But go and learn what this means: 'I desire mercy, and not sacrifice.' For I did not come to call the righteous, but sinners, to repentance.*"

Oral Questions

1. What was the profession of Jesus' first disciples?
2. What did they do when Jesus called them to follow Him?
3. Jesus was going into every part of Galilee; multitudes were follow ing Him. What was He doing to call such attention to Himself?
4. What was the first healing recorded in the Book of Matthew?
5. What was the Roman officer's servant's problem?
6. Where did the demon-possessed men live?
7. What did the demons do when they saw Jesus?
8. What happened to the demons when they left the men?
9. What happened to the pigs?
10. What was the reaction of the owners of the pigs?
11. What kind of man was Matthew?
12. Jesus ate dinner with what kind of people?
13. What did the Pharisees think of this?
14. What kind of answer did Jesus give to the Pharisees?

Spiritual Truths—Lesson 3

Matthew 4-9

Jesus does not make any distinction between people. Jesus' first disciples were fishermen—simple people without formal education. The leper was a person who had been excluded from society because of a skin disease that left him disfigured and despised. The Roman soldier's servant was a crippled person who had no money or position in society. Matthew was a tax collector. He probably was very rich, but he was a corrupt thief. The demon-possessed men were so despised that the townspeople preferred healthy pigs to these men being healed. These men actually had lived among the tombs.

But all these people were important and valuable to Jesus. In the eyes of God you are a person of worth and value. Your past, your finances, your appearance, or your place in society do not mean anything to God. You are valuable because God created you in His image. You have unique value because in love you were created to have a relationship with your Creator—God Himself.

Jesus has power to cure our diseases. In this story what are the examples of people being cured?

Jesus has power over every spirit or demon. Many times, even though they may be trying to do things that are good, some people have become involved with spirts or demons. But before they know what has happened to them, these demons have taken over their lives. These demons follow and torture them and never leave them alone. These people have no power to get rid of these demons from their lives. **Jesus has authority and power over EVERY demon and spirit in the world. ONLY through Jesus Christ can we have freedom from evil spirits.**

Jesus loves people of bad reputation. He accepts all sinners. Jesus does not condemn people, but His desire is to bring every person to repentance and true forgiveness.

The religious people, or Pharisees, did not repent of their sins and thought they were better than the other sinners who were eating with Jesus. <u>What is better: to be a big sinner who has been forgiven or a person with few sins but who refuses to repent?</u>

Being a big sinner who has been forgiven is far better.

Jesus accepts us and loves us just the way we are. Whether we are terrible sinners, are poor, have little education, have lots of problems, or have physical illnesses does not matter. In His eyes we all are the same—we are unique individuals loved by our Creator God. The important thing is for us to repent and follow Him.

The Teachings of Jesus—Lesson 4

Matthew 10-16

"I desire mercy, and not sacrifice" (Mt. 12:7).

Jesus called 12 men to be His disciples—to be close to Him and to be trained by Him. He gave these 12 men power over evil spirits and power to cure all kind of diseases. He told them that they must give freely, for freely they had received. Judas Iscariot was among these men who were sent out.

Jesus sent them to every corner of Israel so they could call the Jewish people to repentance and faith in Jesus Christ. Jesus gave these men a message: *"Whoever confesses Me before men, him I will also confess before My Father who is in heaven. But whoever denies Me before men, him I will also deny before My Father who is in heaven."*

Jesus Himself went all over Galilee; he taught, preached, and healed all kinds of diseases. But the people of Galilee—those with whom He had spent so much of His time—rejected His message. The city of Capernaum, in which He had begun His public ministry, rejected Him. Seeing this, Jesus went to speak to His Father. These were His words:

"I thank you Father, Lord of heaven and earth, that You have hidden these things from the wise and prudent and have revealed them to babes. Even so, Father, for so it seemed good in Your sight. All things have been delivered to me by My Father, and no one knows the Son except the Father. Nor does anyone know the Father, except the Son, and the one to whom the Son wills to reveal Him. Come to Me, all you who labor and are heavy laden, and I will give you rest. Take My yoke upon you and learn from Me, for I am gentle and lowly in heart, and you will find rest for your souls. For My yoke is easy and My burden is light."

After He said these things, Jesus with His disciples went past some wheat fields; this was on a Sabbath. His disciples were hungry, so they stopped, picked some wheat, and ate.

The Pharisees—the religious leaders—saw this and accused them, because working on the Sabbath was against Jewish law. Jesus answered them and said that they still did not understand the law of God, because the Scriptures say, "*I desire mercy, and not sacrifice.*"

From the wheat fields Jesus and the disciples went to the Jewish synagogue; there they met a man with a withered hand. Jesus asked the man to stretch out his hand; in plain view on the Sabbath He cured him there in the synagogue.

The Pharisees, outraged, left that place and formed a council to plot against Jesus to kill Him. Jesus, knowing what they were planning, also left that place. But a multitude followed Him, so He cured all of them and asked them to keep from turning Him in.

Jesus continued working in this region for a while longer; he taught the people and healed their diseases. Twice the people followed Him out into the wilderness and stayed there long stretches of time as they listened to His words without even eating. Twice, Jesus took less than seven loaves of bread and a few fish and fed more than 4,000 people.

While he still was working in Galilee, Jesus explained clearly to His followers that He soon would be going to Jerusalem and that horrible things would happen there. He told them that He would have to suffer many things in the hands of the Jewish leaders and that He would be killed, but that three days later He would rise again unto life.

Oral Questions

1. What was the assignment that Jesus gave His disciples?
2. What did Jesus say He would do for those people who confessed Him before others? What about those who denied Him before other people?
3. How did the inhabitants of Capernaum, as well as many other cities in Galilee in which He had performed most of His miracles, react to Jesus' message?
4. Jesus said he would receive all those who are weary and heavy-

laden. What does He promise to do for these people?

5. Why did Jesus and His disciples stop in the wheat fields?

6. Why were the Pharisees critical of Jesus for gathering wheat?

7. Why were the Pharisees against Jesus healing the man with the withered hand?

8. What was the purpose of the council created by the Jewish leaders?

9. Jesus told His followers that certain things would happen to Him. What was His prophecy?

Spiritual Truths—Lesson 4

Matthew 10-16

1. <u>Those who confess the name of Jesus before others, He will confess before His Father.</u> But those who deny Him before others, He also will deny before His Father in Heaven.

2. <u>Many followed Jesus only because they wanted some miracle from Him, but they did not want a relationship with Him; they did not want to obey His words.</u> They did not want to repent of their sins. They only wanted to take advantage of God's mercy. Today do people still do things such as this?

3. The only person who has access to the Father is Jesus Christ and those who come to the Father through Jesus Christ. <u>Jesus Christ is the only intercessor. Only one God exists; we have only one way to reach Him. The Bible teaches that way is Jesus Christ and Jesus Christ alone.</u>

* Maybe you have been taught to pray to God through other intercessors besides Jesus Christ. Who are these other intercessors? Are they gods, prophets, deceased family members, or good people of the past? The Bible says they may have been good people, but none of these people is God. Do you agree with the Bible that Jesus Christ is the only intercessor between God and others?

4. <u>Jesus wants to carry our burdens and our worries. He is gentle and lowly in heart. Many of us work hard to be good people. We try to follow the correct religious traditions. We try to help the needy and do works that God will review and approve. But trying to please God is a difficult burden; trying to live a good life is a difficult burden; sometimes just living from day to day is a difficult burden.</u>

<u>Jesus Christ</u> wants to relieve us of the weights that we carry. In Him we can find rest for our souls if we accept His yoke. In other words if we accept His Lordship or leadership in our lives, he will relieve the burden and worry of today.

5. <u>Jesus is concerned about our physical needs.</u> The disciples were hungry; Jesus provided food for them, knowing that this would pro-

voke anger and persecution from the Pharisees. <u>The Creator God of the Universe is worried about the physical needs of each of us.</u>

* "*I desire mercy, not sacrifice.*" What does the word *sacrifice* mean to you? Have religious leaders taught you to make sacrifices to God—maybe to receive favor or forgiveness of a sin? Do you have difficulty believing that God does not want you to prove anything to Him by sacrifices? This is the second time that Jesus tried to explain to the Pharisees that God is not pleased with our human sacrifices. But for people who are very religious, this often is a difficult fact to accept. All religions teach that we must do something to avoid the wrath of God or to gain the favor of God. Many people go through many hardships trying to pay God back for promises they've made, pay for past sins, or simply to show loyalty to God. But this proves NOTHING to God. He wants a relationship with us. He wants to show us mercy; He does not want our sacrifices. Jesus knew that He would have to suffer many things and then die. But that after three days He would resurrect from the dead. This all was a part of God's plan. He tried to explain this to His disciples, but they could not understand why He must die and then resurrect.

In the last three lessons of this study we will try to understand the significance of Jesus' death and resurrection. This unique event would change the history of the world forever. This single event has the power to break the bondage of sin and to transform our lives.

Jesus Is Betrayed by Judas—Lesson 5

Matthew 20-26

Now Jesus, going up to Jerusalem, took the twelve disciples aside on the road and said to them, "Behold, we are going up to Jerusalem, and the Son of Man will be betrayed to the chief priests and to the scribes; and they will condemn Him to death, and deliver Him to the Gentiles to mock and to scourge and to crucify. And the third day He will rise again" (Mt. 20:17-19).

Jesus with His disciples made the journey from Galilee to Jerusalem. As He was about to arrive in Jerusalem, Jesus asked two of His disciples to pass by a certain village and to retrieve a donkey and colt that He needed. Jesus sat on this colt for the trip into the city of Jerusalem.

He entered gloriously and triumphantly. A multitude gathered around Him on each side of the street. A large number of people lay their own clothes on the road to make a type of carpet for Jesus to enter into the city. Some people broke palm branches and spread them all over the road as a means of honoring Him. Still others would walk before and behind Him yelling, *"Hosanna to the Son of David! Blessed is He who comes in the Name of the LORD! Hosanna in the highest!"*

The entire city of Jerusalem was moved by this grand and unusual event. Everyone in town was asking, "Who is this?" So many people answered, "This is Jesus, the prophet from Nazareth of Galilee."

So Jesus entered the city and went to the Jewish temple. There he kicked out all of the vendors; He overturned the tables of the money-changers who had set up booths in the temple. He said to them, *"It is written, MY house shall be called a house of prayer, but you have made it a den of thieves."* After this He stayed in the temple healing the blind and the lame.

After Jesus had taught the people many things and performed

many signs and wonders in the temple, the chief priests and the religious leaders joined together to plot His death. They discussed how someway by trickery they might kill Him. They were, however, anxious about executing such a plot during the Passover, so they decided to wait until the Passover was over to deal with Jesus.

One of the 12 disciples, Judas Iscariot, went to meet the chief priests and said, *"What are you willing to give me if I deliver Him to you?"* They agreed and gave him 30 silver coins. From that time on Judas began to look for an opportunity in which he might betray Jesus.

Since the week was that of the Passover, the disciples prepared the dinner for the feast according to specific instructions given by Jesus. On the night of the celebration Jesus sat down together with the 12 disciples and said to them, *"Assuredly I say to you, one of you will betray Me."* As He said this, the disciples became very sad. Each of them began asking, *"Lord, is it I?"*

Jesus answered them by saying; *"He who dipped his hand with Me in the dish will betray Me. The Son of Man indeed goes just as it is written of Him, but woe to that man by whom the Son of Man is betrayed! It would have been good for that man if he had not been born."*

Judas, the one who was betraying Him, asked, *"Rabbi, is it I?"* Jesus answered him, *"You have said it."*

They all ate dinner together that evening. While they were eating, Jesus took bread, blessed, broke it, and said, *"Take, eat; this is My body."* Then He took the cup, gave thanks, gave it to them, and said, *"Drink from it, all of you. For this is My blood of the new covenant, which is shed for many for the remission of sins."*

After they finished the meal, they sang a hymn and together went to the hill called Mount of Olives. There Jesus continued to teach them many things, some of which were about the events that would happen soon.

Then Jesus brought them down to a place called Gethsemane, at which they were to pray with Him all night long. Jesus took Peter, James, and John with Him as He began to become deeply distressed. He asked them to please sit up with Him. He then left them and went a little farther away to pray to His Father alone. He prayed about the things that would unfold soon. He prayed these words: *"O My Father, if it is possible, let this cup pass from Me; nevertheless, not as I will, but as You will."* Three times He prayed this same prayer; He was extremely sad.

The disciples, however, could not even keep their eyes open for a single hour. They all fell asleep. Finally, Jesus woke them all up and said, *"Rise, let us be going. See, My betrayer is at hand."*

Oral Questions

1. On what kind of animal did Jesus enter Jerusalem?
2. How did the people treat Jesus as He was entering into the city?
3. What did Judas do to betray Jesus?
4. What festival was being celebrated in the city?
5. How did Jesus warn Judas that He knew He would betray Him?
6. What did Jesus say about the wine at the supper?
7. According to Jesus, for what is the shedding of blood necessary?
8. Jesus took His disciples to Gethsemane to spend the night in prayer. How many of His disciples were able to stay up all night praying?
9. What was the prayer that Jesus prayed the night of His betrayal?

Spiritual Truths—Lesson 5

Matthew 20-26

1. <u>God is in control of all things.</u> The Pharisees were conspiring to catch Jesus by surprise. But the entire time God was using them to exercise His perfect will on earth. God's will always was that Jesus would die on the cross.

2. <u>God knows what is in our hearts—things others don't know.</u> The entire time Jesus knew that His disciple, Judas, was going to betray Him.

3. <u>Jesus loves us and treats us with the same love even if we reject Him.</u> Jesus treated Judas so well that no other disciple could believe he was the traitor. In the same way Jesus loves us and treats us lovingly even though many times we betray and reject Him and His will for our lives.

4. <u>The blood of Jesus was shed for us for the remission or forgiveness of our sins.</u> At the time the disciples did not understand the fact that Jesus had to die. They did not understand that God demands of all people the payment of sins in their lives and that this payment is the shedding of blood. They understood that Jesus loved them and that they were forgiven of their sins. But they would need more time until they understood the price that Jesus had to pay to be able to forgive their sins.

* Many people know that they have sin in their lives. Some people even may have heard the story of Jesus and that He loves them. But very few understand that God demands blood as a payment for sin. Jesus, because He is God, is the only person who ever has lived or will live on this earth who did not commit a single sin. Because of His incredible love for us He chose to surrender His life as a sacrifice to pay the price for our sins—not just ours but for the sins of the whole world. Because of this sacrifice we now have an opportunity to receive forgiveness for our sins and peace with God.

Next week we will look at the details of the crucifixion of Christ.

The Crucifixion of Jesus—Lesson 6

Matthew 26-27

Jesus said to him, "It is as you said. Nevertheless, I say to you here-after you will see the Son of Man sitting at the right hand of the Power, and coming on the clouds of heaven" (Mt. 26:64.)

While still was waking His disciples, Judas, the one who had be-trayed Him, arrived with a large group of people, including the chief priests and religious leaders. Many carried swords and clubs. Judas ap-proached Jesus and kissed Him as he said, *"Greetings, Rabbi!"* Jesus answered Him, *"Friend, why have you come?"*

Suddenly one of Jesus' disciples rashly pulled out a sword and cut off the ear of one of the chief priest's servants. Jesus corrected the dis-ciple and healed the man's ear. He informed this disciple that if He so desired, 12 legions of angels stood by ready to do battle, but all was occurring so that the Scriptures could be fulfilled.

Jesus then turned to the gang of people that had arrived and asked them, *"Have you come out, as against a robber, with swords and clubs to take Me? I sat daily with you, teaching in the temple, and you did not seize Me. But all this was done that the Scriptures of the prophets might be fulfilled."* His disciples quickly fled from that place and left Him alone.

Those who had seized Him took Him to the house of a man named Caiaphas, who at the time was the highest priest. All the priests and re-ligious leaders who were ready to interrogate Jesus waited there. They had arranged for many false witnesses to testify against Him to con-demn Him to death. Many testified, but even still they could not gather sufficient evidence to put Him to death until the high priest himself began to interrogate Him. He finally asked Jesus, *"I put You under oath by the living God: Tell us if You are the Christ, the Son of God!"*

Jesus said to him, *"It is as you said. Nevertheless, I say to you, hereafter you will see the Son of Man sitting at the right hand of the Power, and coming on the clouds of heaven."*

Hearing this answer the chief priest ripped off his clothes and said, *"Blasphemy!"* The people that had gathered there then took Jesus and began to spit on His face. Some beat Him, while others struck Him with the palms of their hands and said, *"Prophesy to us, Christ! Who is the one who struck You?"*

When morning finally arrived, the priests and religious leaders took Jesus to the region's Roman governor named Pontius Pilate. They told Pilate that Jesus claimed to be the King of the Jews. Pilate interrogated Jesus and asked Him, *"Are You the King of the Jews?"* Jesus answered, *"It is as you say."*

But even after all of his interrogation Pilate could not find a reason to crucify Jesus Also, the previous night, Pilate's wife had had a disturbing dream about the whole thing and warned her husband to have nothing to do with Jesus. Pilate knew that the Jewish leaders had turned Jesus into him only out of envy, but the governor did not know what to do, since the people had become stirred up.

Every year at Passover time Pilate's custom was to release one prisoner of the people's choice. This year an especially notorious criminal named Barabbas was in jail. Pilate produced both Barabbas and Jesus and made an offer to the people: *"Whom do you want me to release to you? Barabbas or Jesus, who is called Christ?"* But the people, who had been riled up by the Pharisees, yelled out, *"Barabbas!"*

"What then shall I do with Jesus who is called Christ?" asked Pilate. The people cried out, *"Let Him be crucified."*

So Pilate, seeing that the people were beginning to riot, got a basin of water and washed his hands. He said, *"I am innocent of the blood of this just Person, you see to it."* He released Barabbas to the people and sent Jesus to be whipped.

Pilate's soldiers took Jesus to Pilate's headquarters, the Praetorium, where they tortured and mocked Him. They gathered all around Him, stripped Him, and dressed Him in a scarlet robe. Then they twisted a crown of thorns and put it into His head. They gave Him a reed to hold as if it was a scepter. They kneeled in front of Him sarcastically and said, *"Hail, King of the Jews!"* They spat on Him; they then took the reed that had been in His hand and hit Him on the head with it. After they had finished making fun of Him, they took the robe off, put His clothes back on Him, and led Him away to the place called Golgotha, or the "Place of a Skull"—the place at which He was to be crucified.

On the cross on which they crucified Him, the Romans put a plaque over His head. It read, *"This is Jesus the King of the Jews."* Jesus was crucified between two thieves—one on either side of Him.

From the sixth hour to the ninth hour, while Jesus was hanging on the cross, a great darkness covered all the land. About the ninth hour, Jesus cried out and said, *"Eli Eli, lama sabachthani?"* This means, *"My God, My God, why have You forsaken Me?"* A little later He yelled again. With this yell He surrendered His Spirit.

At the time that He surrendered His Spirit, many bizarre things occurred simultaneously. The veil of the temple was torn in two from top to bottom, the earth quaked, many rocks split, and many graves were opened, so that many bodies of saints who had fallen asleep were raised. These bodies, after His resurrection, left their graves, went into Jerusalem, and were seen by many people.

Oral Questions

1. How was Jesus betrayed?
2. To try to defend Jesus, one of Jesus' disciples did something very radical. What was it? What was Jesus' reaction?
3. At the time of His betrayal what did all of His disciples do?
4. Where did the men from the garden take Jesus?
5. Even though many false witnesses arose, how was Jesus eventually convicted of blasphemy?
6. As soon as morning broke, where did the Jewish leaders take Jesus?
7. Pilate, after his interrogation, did not find Jesus guilty but was afraid of the people, so he gave the people a choice. What was the offer he made the people? What was the people's choice?
8. How did the soldiers treat Jesus?
9. After three hours of darkness, Jesus yelled out to God. What is the translation of this yell?
10. What were some of the unusual things that happened when Jesus surrendered His Spirit?

Spiritual Truths—Lesson 6

Matthew 26-27

1. Who is Jesus? *"The Son of Man sitting at the right hand of the Power, and coming on the clouds of heaven."* This was the answer Jesus gave the chief priest; this response ultimately led to His crucifixion. Those people could not accept this answer. But each of us also must wrestle with this same question: *Who really is Jesus?* Because if Jesus really is *sitting at the right hand of the Power, and coming on the clouds of heaven,* we each must decide how we will respond to Him.

2. Jesus was crucified in the place of Barabbas, a despised criminal; in turn Barabbas was set free.

Maybe I am not a despised criminal, but just like Barabbas I am a sinner. Before God I, too, have earned a death penalty. In Romans 6:23 the Bible says, *The wages of sin is death.* This means that we all deserve to die because of the bad things that we have done in our lives. Whether we have many sins, as in the case of Barabbas, or whether we have been relatively good people, as some of His disciples had been, does not matter. Whether we have done more deeds than bad deeds does not matter. Our good deeds have no power to erase the sin in our lives.

3. Jesus was tortured, judged, and killed to pay the penalty for the sins in our lives. This was the reason Jesus was sent to earth. He wanted us to be people who have been forgiven of our sins when we stand before God. Some people have said that Jesus was a martyr or a prophet. But according to Jesus' own confession this is not true. He claimed to be God and to have been sent to earth to die for our sins. Only the blood of Jesus can eliminate sin.

4. Jesus surrendered His Spirit. At any moment Jesus could have de-scended from the cross. With a single word He could have killed all of the people who made fun of Him. But by His own choosing He endured the humiliation and stayed on the cross until the chosen hour. Then in His time He surrendered His Spirit. He chose to die because

He wanted to pay the debt for our sins. In John 3:16 the Bible says, *"God so loved the world that He gave His only begotten Son, that whosoever believes on Him will not perish but have everlasting life."* This verse means that believing in Jesus can bring forgiveness of sin. This verse says that believing in Jesus can give us the assurance of everlasting life.

In the next lesson we will study the resurrection of Jesus. The truth is that Jesus is not dead but is alive and today wants to enter your life. He wants to purify your heart from all your sins and to transform your life completely.

The Resurrection of Jesus—Lesson 7

Matthew 27-28

"Do not be afraid, for I know that you seek Jesus who was crucified. He is not here; for He is risen, as He said" (Mt. 28:5-6).

A very rich man named Joseph of Arimathea also was a disciple of Jesus. Joseph asked Pilate for permission to take Jesus' body and place Him in his own tomb. Pilate agreed; Jesus was laid in a new tomb. Afterward, a great rock was rolled against the door of the tomb.

The next day the Pharisees met together and went before Pilate, because they remembered the words of Jesus when He said that He would rise again on the third day. They asked Pilate whether He would make the tomb secure until the third day in case something should happen to the body. So Pilate gave them permission to make it as secure as they knew how. They went to the place, put guards in front of the tomb, and sealed the stone.

On the first day of the week Mary Magdalene and the other Mary went to the tomb in which Jesus lay. When they got there, an earthquake occurred, the rock that had been used to seal the tomb was moved, and an angel of the Lord sat on the stone. The guards that had been protecting the tomb shook in fear and had become like dead men.

The angel told the women, *"Do not be afraid, for I know that you seek Jesus who was crucified. He is not here; for He is risen, as He said. Come see the place where the Lord lay. And go quickly and tell His disciples that He is risen from the dead, and indeed He is going before you into Galilee; there you will see Him. Behold, I have told you."*

With fear and great joy the women ran out of the tomb and hurried to tell the disciples what had happened. But as they went to find the disciples, Jesus met them and said, *"Rejoice!"* They stopped, held Him by the feet, and worshiped Him. He told them to tell the disciples to meet Him in Galilee.

The soldiers who had guarded the tomb entered the city and told the high priests what had happened at the tomb. The high priests consulted each other and decided to give the soldiers a large sum of money. They wanted the soldiers to spread the word that the disciples had stolen the body while the soldiers had fallen asleep on the site. They further promised the guards that if word got to Pilate that they had gone to sleep, then they themselves personally would defend the soldiers in front of the governor. So the soldiers took the bribe and spread many rumors that for several years circulated around the city.

The 11 remaining disciples went to Galilee to the mountain on which Jesus had told them to meet Him. When they saw Him, they all worshiped Him, but some doubted.

So Jesus, speaking to them for the last time, said, *"All authority has been given to Me in heaven and on earth. Go therefore and make disciples of all the nations, baptizing them in the name of the Father and of the Son and of the Holy Spirit, teaching them to observe all things that I have commanded you; and lo, I am with you always, even to the end of the age."*

Oral Questions

1. What did Joseph of Arimathea ask of Pilate?
2. The Pharisees were afraid that on the third day something would happen to Jesus' body. Why?
3. On the first day who went to see Jesus? When the women arrived at the tomb, what did these women find?
4. While they returned to tell the disciples what they had discovered, whom did they encounter?
5. Jesus told his disciples to meet them at another place besides Jerusalem. Where was this place?
6. On the mountain Jesus had a very important command to give His disciples. Try to fill in the blanks with Jesus' words: *"Go, therefore and make _____ of all nations, _____ them in the name of the Father, the Son and the _____ _____, teaching them to observe all things that I have commanded you, and lo, I am with you always, even to the end of the age."*

Spiritual Truths—Lesson 7

Matthew 27-28

1. Jesus is alive today. <u>Jesus is not a human being who can be imprisoned and killed. He is God eternal.</u> He is without beginning and without end. From the beginning of the world God's plan was for Him to be sent to earth in the form of a man who would be a suffering servant. His will was to be crucified on that day and in that way. His plans cannot be frustrated, nor can anyone ever prevail over Him. He still is and always will be God—the only true living God.

2. The Pharisees believed the words of Jesus to the point that they had soldiers guarding His tomb after His death because He had promised to rise again. They believed the words of the soldiers when they told them what had happened. They even paid the soldiers to lie about this event. These same leaders had been present when John the Baptist baptized Jesus and when God's very own voice spoke from heaven and confirmed who He was. These men were witnesses to many of the miracles that He performed. They even were angry with Him when on the Sabbath He cured the man with the withered hand. They had seen Him expel from tormented people many demons; they had watched Him forgive people of their sins. Almost no one knew more about the life and message of Jesus than did the Pharisees. But this same group of people did not accept the love of God that He offered in their own lives. They did not repent of their sins. They did not surrender the control of their lives to the authority of Jesus Christ. <u>To have a relationship with Jesus Christ is more than learning and believing the facts of His life. It is more than a new and different religion. Jesus desires for us to repent of our sins, believe in Him, and give Him our lives. He wants to become the Lord or leader of our lives. He wants to control us every single day of our lives.</u>

3. Who is Jesus?

   • Jesus was born of a virgin.

- Jesus claimed He was God.
- Jesus performed many miracles and forgave the people who repented of their sins.
- Jesus died on the cross to pay the price for the sins in our lives before a just God.
- Jesus resurrected from the dead and is alive today.
- Jesus wants for me also to repent of my sins and give my life to Him.

The Bible teaches us that Jesus did not die to become an example; He died to be a replacement for you and me. We deserve to face God for all the things that we have done wrong in our lives.

The Bible says, *All who call upon the name of the Lord will be saved* (Rom. 10:13).

- This means that regardless of my past, I can ask Jesus to enter my life. He will forgive me of all my sins and live in my life.

- This also means that from the moment that Jesus enters into my heart, all my past, present, and future sins are ALREADY forgiven before God. This is not because of anything that I have done. It is not because I have chosen a good religion. It is not because I have become a moral person. It is not because my parents are from a specific ethnic group or social class. It is ONLY because I have accepted the sacrifice that Jesus already paid when He died on the cross.

- This means that from this moment on, I am a pure person again in the Eyes of God. I am free from guilt from past wrongdoings. I am free from the burden of trying to please God. I am free from the sins of my past. The Bible teaches that the wages of sin are death, but the death of Christ is enough to make me a new creature, if I make the choice to follow Him.

If you would like the forgiveness of God right now in your life, and would like to become a follower of Christ, you may ask Him to enter into your heart right this moment. You do not have to physically be in any particular religious place; you do not have to say any special or magic words. Approaching God and declaring that you believe that Jesus is God and that you want Him to be the Lord or controller of your life is all that is important.

Would you like to confess Jesus as the Lord and Savior of your life?

If your answer is *yes*, just tell Him this. Talking to God is called *prayer*. Pray to Jesus; tell Him you believe He is the one true God. Tell Him you admit that you, too, are a sinner and need the forgiveness of Jesus in your life.

The following prayer is a guide. You may pray this prayer from your heart, or you may use your own words. Specific words are not important; our attitudes and honesty before God is what He desires.

"Father, I know that I am a sinner. I believe that Jesus died on the cross and arose from the grave to save me from my sins. I repent of my sins. Enter into my life and forgive me of all my sins. I give you my life. Thank you for your love for me. In Jesus' name. Amen."

4. *"And lo, I am with you always, even to the end of the age."*

In John 14:2 the Bible says, *"In My Father's house are many mansions; if it were not so, I would have told you. I go to prepare a place for you. And if I go to prepare a place for you, I will come again and receive you to Myself; that where I am, there you may be also."*

Jesus promised us that EVERYONE who gives his or her life to Him will spend eternity with Him in a place called *heaven*. Heaven is the home of the Father. *Once we have accepted Jesus into our lives, we will spend eternity with Jesus*. This means that Jesus will be with us here on earth, but when we die, we will spend eternity with Him in heaven. *We do not have to question whether we will go to heaven. This is a promise of God to everyone who surrenders his life to Jesus Christ.*

The love that Jesus has for us truly lasts forever!

Six Verses that Explain the Gospel

The Presentation of the Gospel

(These six verses explain the essence of the gospel.)

1. The purpose of God for your life

In 1 John 5:13 the Bible says, *I write these things to you who believe in the name of the Son of God so that you may know that you have eternal life.*

Purpose of the verse: To show that, because of His love for us, God wants to give assurance of eternal life.

Explanation of the verse: Eternal life is two things:
a) To know Jesus Christ and have His peace in your heart now while you live in this life (John 17:3).
b) To live with Jesus Christ in heaven for eternity after you die (John 14:1-3).

Application of the verse: Do you want to have assurance that you have eternal life?

Observe: in Christian and non-Christian based cultures these terms will need to be defined clearly. This may take lots of time.

2. Your need

In Romans 3:23 *the Bible says for all have sinned and fall short of the glory of God.*

Purpose of the verse: To show that all of us are sinners.

Explanation of the verse: What is sin? Sin is disobeying God. For example all of us have committed sins such as lying, anger, bitterness, greed, lust, and pride.

Application of the verse: Do you recognize that you have sinned? What is the consequence of sin?

In Romans 6:23 the Bible says, *For the wages of sin is death, but the gift of God is eternal life in Christ Jesus our Lord.*

Purpose of the verse: To show that all deserve death because of our sins.

Explanation of the verse: What is *death*? Death means to be separated from God in two ways.

> First, death is separation from God now in this life on earth. It is a life without joy or peace in the soul. It is a life without assurance of eternal life and without Jesus in your heart. Separation from God leaves us with empty and fearful hearts.

> Second, death is separation from God for eternity in hell. This is a life without Christ for all eternity. According to the Bible all of us deserve death—separation from God—because of our sins.

Application of the verse: Do you understand that you deserve death—separation from God—because of your sins?

3. The provision of God

In Romans 5:8 the Bible says, *But God demonstrates his own love to us in this: while we were still sinners, Christ died for us.*

Purpose of the verse: To show that God loves us so much that He gave

His Son Jesus Christ to die for our sins.

Explanation of the verse: The only payment for sin is death. Jesus Christ was punished, judged, and condemned to death on the cross to pay the penalty of sin in our place.

The death of Jesus was the only sacrifice that was sufficient to free us of the guilt of sin. Many people are trying to get to God through different ways: depending on their own good life or good works. They also may try to get to God through saints, idols, images, spirits, or reincarnation.

Our own efforts have no power to purify us of our sins. The only way to have a relationship with God is through Jesus Christ. After Jesus Christ died on the cross for our sins, He arose from the dead and conquered death. He is alive and wants to live in your heart.

Application of the verse: Do you believe that Jesus Christ is your only Lord, Savior, and Mediator?

4. Your response

In Romans 10: 9 the Bible says, *That if you confess with your mouth, "Jesus is Lord", and believe in your heart that God raised him from the dead, you will be saved.*

Purpose of the verse: To show what you do to receive Jesus as your Lord.

Explanation of the verse: To receive Jesus do two things:
a) First, to receive Jesus, confess Christ as your only Lord. Abandon your sins and turn to follow Jesus. This means to turn the control of your life over to Christ. This is repentance.
b) Second, to receive Jesus, believe in your heart that Christ rose from the dead and is your only Savior. This means that you

have to stop putting your faith in other things like morality, good works, idols, images, saints, or reincarnation and put your trust in Jesus Christ as your only Savior.

Application of the verse: Are you ready to confess Jesus as Lord and give your life to Jesus as your only Lord? Are you ready to stop putting your faith in other things and give your life to Christ right now as your only Lord and Savior?

In Romans 10:13 the Bible says, *"Everyone who calls on the name of the Lord will be saved."*

Purpose of the verse: To show that anyone that calls on the name of Jesus will be saved.

Explanation of the verse: This means that right now in your heart you can accept Jesus by faith.

Application of the verse: Are you ready to give your life to Jesus and to ask Him to enter in your life right now? If you are ready, with all your heart say this prayer to God.

> *"Lord, I am a sinner. I trust in you, Lord, as my only Lord, Savior, and Mediator. I give my life to You. Please enter my heart and save me right now. Transform me and take full control of my life. Amen."*

Do you believe that Jesus answered your prayer? Then where is Jesus right now? Are you saved?

Footnotes

[1]Spencer, *The Truth about Muhammad*, p. 35.

[2]Harris, *How to Lead Muslims to Christ*, p. 88.

[3]Ibid., p. 88.

[4]Braswell, *What We Need to Know about Islam and Muslims*, p. 12.

[5]Harris, p. 88.

[6]Bukhari, Hadith Sahih. Vol. 6, Book 65, no. 4953, in Spencer, *The Truth about Muhammad*, p. 42.

[7]Ishaq, Ibn. *The Life of Muhammad: A Translation of Ibn Ishaq's Sirat Rasul Allah*, p. 106 in Spencer, *The Truth about Muhammad*, p. 42.

[8]Spencer, *The Truth about Muhammad*, p. 42.

[9]Ishaq, Ibn. in Spencer, *The Truth about Muhammad*, p. 42.

[10]Spencer, *The Truth about Muhammad*, p. 44.

[11]Ishaq, Ibn. in Spencer, *The Truth about Muhammad*, p. 45.

[12]Caner, Ergun Mehmet and Emir Fethi Caner, *Unveiling Islam*, p. 42.

[13]Braswell, *Islam*, p. 15.

[14]Rhodes. *Reasoning from the Scriptures with Muslims*, p. 15.

[15]Braswell, *Islam*, p. 15.

[16]Richardson, *Secrets of the Koran*, pp. 32-35.

[17]Geisler and Saleeb, *Answering Islam*, p. 75.

[18]Harris, p. 91.

[19]Warraq, *Why I Am Not a Muslim*, p. 92.

[20]Spencer, *The Politically Incorrect Guide to Islam*, pp. 5-7.

[21]Harris, p. 91.

[22]Warraq, p. 93.

[23]Spencer, *The Truth about Muhammad*, p. 103.

[24]Geisler and Saleeb, p. 77.

[25]Caner, p. 52.

[26]Braswell, *Islam,* p. 18.

[27]Caner, p. 60.

[28]Braswell, *Islam,* p. 18.

[29]Geisler and Saleeb, p. 80.

[30]Geisler and Saleeb, p. 99.

[31]Ibid., pp. 89-90.

[32]Spencer, *The Complete Infidel's Guide to the Koran*, pp. 30-31.

[33]Bukhari, Hadith Sahih. Vol. 6, Book 65, no. 4953, in Spencer, *The Complete Infidel's Guide to the Koran*, p. 37.

[34]Geisler and Saleeb, p. 94.

[35]Ibid., p. 94.

[36]Ibid., p. 96.

[37]Rhodes, *The 10 Things You Need to Know about Islam*, p. 26.

[38]Spencer, *The Complete Infidel's Guide to the Koran*, p. 237.

[39]Mawdudi, *The Islamic Movement*, p. 31-32 in Zeidan, *Sword of Allah*, pp. 68-69.

[40]Braswell, *Islam*, pp. 119-120.

[41]Rhodes, *The 10 Things You Need to Know About Islam*, pp. 64-66.

[42]Braswell, *What You Need to Know about Islam & Muslims*, pp. 34-35.

[43]Ibid., p. 35.

[44]Rhodes, *The 10 Things You Need to Know about Islam*, p. 67.

[45]Ibid., p. 68.

[46]Braswell, *What You Need to Know about Islam & Muslims*, pp. 36-37.

[47]Ankerberg, *The Facts on Islam*, p. 11.

[48]Braswell, *What You Need to Know about Islam & Muslims*, p. 37.

[49]Ibid., p. 37.

[50]George, *Is the Father of Jesus the God of Muhammad?*, p. 50.

[51]Braswell, *What You Need to Know about Islam & Muslims*, p. 38.

[52]Ibid., p. 38.

[53]Caner, p. 49.

[54]Spencer, *The Politically Incorrect Guide to Islam*, p. 10.

[55]Spencer, p. 24.

[56]Braswell, *What You Need to Know about Islam & Muslims*, p. 39.

[57]Braswell, *Islam*, p. 48.

[58]Ibid., p. 49.

[59]Ankerberg, *The Facts on Islam*, p. 10.

[60]Braswell, *Islam*, p. 50.

[61]Ibid., p. 50.

[62]Ankerberg, *The Facts on Islam*, p. 10.

[63]Braswell, *Islam*, p. 20.

[64]Braswell, *What You Need to Know about Islam & Muslims*, p. 109.

[65]Ibid., p. 109.

[66]Rhodes, *Reasoning from the Scriptures with Muslims*, p. 132.

[67]Ibid., p. 132.

[68]Braswell, *What You Need to Know about Islam & Muslims*, p. 111.

[69]Rhodes, *Reasoning from the Scriptures with Muslims*, p. 133.

[70]Ibid., p. 134.

[71]Ibid., p. 136.

[72]Ali, *The Meaning of The Holy Qur'an*, p. 1182.

[73]Geisler and Saleeb, p. 18.

[74]Braswell, *Islam*, p. 57.

[75]Ankerberg, p. 18.

[76]Braswell, *What You Need to Know About Islam & Muslims*, pp. 25-26.

[77]Rhodes, The 10 Things You Need to Know about Islam, p. 88.

[78]Ali, p. 759.

[79]Rhodes, *Reasoning from the Scriptures with Muslims*, p. 258.

[80]Greenson, *Camel Training Manual*, p. 48.

[81]Braswell, *What You Need to Know about Islam & Muslims*, p. 77.

[82]Hoskins, *A Muslim's Heart*, p. 18.

[83]Ibid., p. 18.

[84]Ibid., p. 20.

[85]Braswell, *What You Need to Know about Islam & Muslims*, p. 78.

[86]Akins, *Pioneer Evangelism*, pp. 54-55.

[87]MacArthur, *The MacArthur Study Bible*, p. 1612.

[88]Akins, *Pioneer Evangelism*, pp. 56-57.

[89]Yousef, *Son of Hamas*, p. 122.

[90]Akins, *Pioneer Evangelism*, pp. 80-81.

[91]Rutledge, *In the Presence of Mine Enemies*, p. 25.

[92]Barclay, *New Testament Words*, p. 168.

[93]Wuest, *Wuest's Studies from the New Testament Greek*, p. 82.

[94]Robertson, *Word Pictures in the New Testament*, Vol. IV, p. 357.

[95]Souza, *Regard sur Ouidah, A Bit of History*, pp. 35-39.

[96]Wuest, *Romans in the Greek New Testament, Wuest's Word Studies for the English Reader*, p. 67.

[97]Akins, *Be a 24/7 Christian*, pp. 43-54.

[98]Strong, *Systematic Theology*, pp. 837-838.

[99]MacArthur, *The Gospel According to the Apostles*, p. 23.

[100]Ibid., p. 30.

[101]Warren, *The Purpose Driven Life*, p. 78.

[102]Marsh, *Share Your Faith with a Muslim*, p. 26.

Bibliography

Adams, Moody, 2004. *The Koran: with Commentary,* Baton Rouge, LA: M. A. E. Association.

Akins, Thomas Wade, 2005. *Be a 24/7 Christian,* Garland, TX: Hannibal Books.

Akins, Thomas Wade, 2006. *Pioneer Evangelism,* Rio de Janeiro, Brazil: Junta De Missoes Nacionas.

Ali, Abdullah Yusuf, 1409. *The Meaning of The Holy Qur'an,* Beltsville, MD: Amana Publications.

Ankerberg, John and John Weldon, 1998. *The Facts on Islam: Answers to the Most Frequently Asked Questions,* Eugene, OR: Harvest House Publishers.

Barclay, William, 1974. *New Testament Words,* Philadelphia, PA: Westminster Press.

Braswell, George W., Jr., 1996. *Islam: Its Prophet, Peoples, Politics, and Power,* Nashville, TN: Broadman and Holman Publishers.

Braswell, George. W., Jr., 2000. *What You Need to Know about Islam & Muslims,* Nashville, TN: Broadman and Holman Publishers.

Caner, Ergun Mehmet and Emir Fethi Caner, 2002. *Unveiling Islam: An Insider's Look at Muslim Life and Beliefs,* Grand Rapids, MI: Kregel Publications.

Crosby, Fanny J. *Redeemed.*

Gabriel, Brigitte, 2008. *They Must Be Stopped: Why We Must Defeat Radical Islam and How We Can Do It,* New York, NY: St. Martin's Press.

Geisler, Norman L. and Abdul Saleeb, 1993. *Islam: The Crescent in the Light of the Cross,* Grand Rapids, MI: Baker Books.

George, Timothy, 2002. *Is the Father of Jesus the God of Muhammad?: Understanding the Differences between Christianity and Islam,* Grand Rapids, MI: Zondervan.

Greenson, Kevin, 2004. *Camel Training Manual,* Bangalore, India: Wigtake Resources.

Harris, Geo. K., 1957. *How to Lead Muslims to Christ: A Concise Manual,* Philadelphia, PA: China Inland Mission.

Hoskins, Edward J., M.D., Ph.D., 2003. *A Muslim's Heart: What Every Christian Needs to Know to Share Christ with Muslims,* Colorado Springs, CO: Dawson Media.

Ibn Ishaq, 1955. *The Life of Muhammad: A Translation of Ibn Ishaq's Sirat Rasul Allah,* A. Guillaume, translator. Oxford, England: Oxford University Press.

MacArthur, John, Ph.D., 1993. *The Gospel According to the Apostles,* Word Publishing.

MacArthur, John, 1997. *The MacArthur Study Bible,* Dallas, TX: Thomas Nelson, Inc.

Marsh, Charles R., 1975. *Share Your Faith with a Muslim,* Chicago, IL: Moody Press.

Morey, Robert A., 1992. *Islamic Invasion,* Eugene, OR: Harvest House Publishers.

Rhodes, Ron, 2002. *Reasoning from the Scriptures with Muslims,* Eugene, OR: Harvest House Publishers.

Rhodes, Ron, 2007. *The 10 Things You Need to Know about Islam,* Eugene, OR: Harvest House Publishers.

Richardson, Don, 2003. *Secrets of the Koran: Revealing Insights into Islam's Holy Book,* Ventura, CA: Regal Books.

Robertson, Archibald Thomas, 1931. *Word Pictures in the New Testament, Vol. IV,* Grand Rapids: Baker Book House.

Rushdie, Salman, 1989. *The Satanic Verses,* New York, NY: Viking Penguin.

Rutledge, Howard and Phyllis, 1973. *In the Presence of Mine Enemies.* Old Tappan, NJ: Fleming H. Revell.

Parshall, Phil, 2002. *The Cross and the Crescent: Understanding the Muslim Heart and Mind,* Waynesboro, GA: Gabriel Publishing.

Saal, William J., 1991. *Reaching Muslims for Christ,* Chicago, IL: Moody Press.

Shoebat, Walid, 2005. *Why I Left Jihad, The Root of Terrorism and the Return of*

Radical Islam, United States of America: Top Executive Media.

Shorrosh, Anis A., Dr., 1988. *Islam Revealed: A Christian Arab's View of Islam*, Nashville, TN: Thomas Nelson, Inc.

Souza, Martine de. *Regard sur Ouidah, A Bit of History,* Ouidah, Benin, Africa.

Spencer, Robert, 2005. *The Politically Incorrect Guide to Islam (and the Crusades),* Washington, DC: Regnery Publishing, Inc.

Spencer, Robert, 2006. *The Truth about Muhammad: Founder of the World's Most Intolerant Religion*, Washington, DC: Regnery Publishing, Inc.

Spencer, Robert, 2008. *Stealth Jihad: How Radical Islam Is Subverting America without Guns or Bombs*, Washington, DC: Regnery Publishing, Inc.

Spencer, Robert, 2009. *The Complete Infidel's Guide to the Koran*, Washington, DC: Regnery Publishing, Inc.

Strong, Dr. Augustus H., 1907. *Systematic Theology*, Philadelphia: Judson. 837-838.

Swartley, Keith E., 2005. *Encountering the World of Islam*, Waynesboro, GA: Authentic.

Warraq, Ibn, 1995. *Why I Am Not a Muslim*, Amherst, New York: Prometheus Books.

Warren, Rick, 2002. *The Purpose Driven Life*, Grand Rapids, MI: Zondervan.

Wuest, Kenneth S., 1953. *Wuest's Studies from the New Testament Greek*. Grand Rapids, MI: Wm. B. Eerdmans Publishing.

Wuest, Kenneth S., 1955. *Romans in the Greek New Testament, Wuest's Word Studies for the English Reader,* Grand Rapids, MI: Wm. B. Eerdmans Publishing.

Yousef, Mosab Hassan, 2010. *Son of Hamas: A Gripping Account of Terror, Betrayal, Political Intrigue, and Unthinkable Choices*, Carol Stream, IL: Tyndale House Publishers, Inc.

Zeidan, David, 2003. *Sword of Allah: Islamic Fundamentalism from an Evangelical Perspective,* Waynesboro, GA: Gabriel Publishing.

TO CONTACT THE AUTHOR
WRITE TO HIM AT
www.pioneermissions.org

Other Missions Titles from Hannibal Books

Be a 24/7 Christian by Wade Akins. Want to make Jesus truly the Lord of your life but don't know how? This renowned missionary evangelist/strategist tells how to live the adventure of being totally sold out to the Lord every moment of every day, every day of every year.

_____**Copies at $12.95=**_____

How to Be Spiritual without Being Weird by Christy Akins Brawner. Can you live a balanced, meaningful Christian life while still being "hip"? Contemporary young people who seek answers for crucial life questions need look no further than this sparkling, authentic Christian apologetic by Christy Brawner, daughter of *Sharing Your Faith with Muslims* author Wade Akins. Brawner shares personal experiences to demonstrate 12 core values people need to thrive in the modern world.

_____**Copies at $12.95=**_____

Beyond Surrender by Barbara J. Singerman. A story of one family's quest to bring light to West Africa's darkness. After they surrendered to missions in Benin, Barbara Singerman and her family found communication to be one step above the Dark Ages. Most people never had seen ice; hunters still used crossbows to bring home their evening meal. Singerman illustrates what keeps dedicated missionaries on the field in the face of unthinkable obstacles.

_____**Copies at $14.95=**_____

The Marvel of It All by Joe and Leona Tarry. How can anyone look back on 36 years of experiences that have included broken-down cars, near-fatal traffic accidents, serious illnesses, the near death of a child, and rebuffed efforts at presenting the gospel and truly marvel at God's goodness. Yet that is exactly what Joe and Leona Tarry do in their account of God's provision for them during more than three-and-a-half decades of serving God as career missionaries in Brazil.

_____**Copies at $29.95=**_____

Add $4 shipping for first book, plus $1 for each additional book.

Shipping & Handling _____

Texas residents add 8.25% sales tax _____

TOTAL ENCLOSED_____

check _____ or credit card # _____ exp. date_____

(Visa, MasterCard, Discover, American Express accepted)

Name _____

Address _____ Phone _____

City _____ State _____ Zip _____

See page 2 for address, phone number, email address, and website.